# The Fairy Tale Art of
# JOHN BAUER

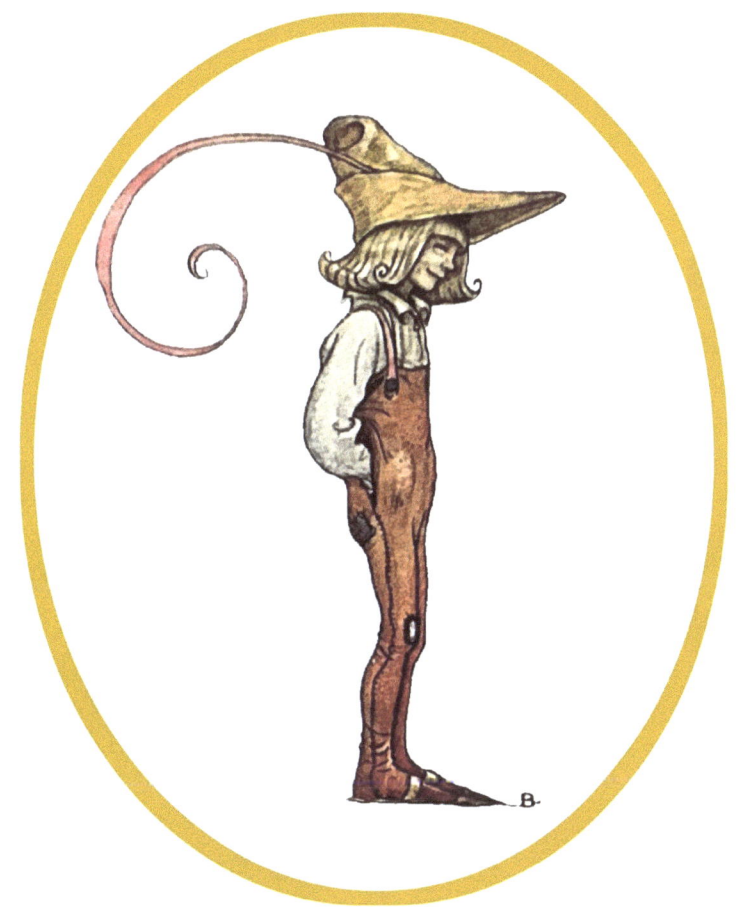

Born in 1882 John Albert Bauer was a Swedish painter and illustrator. He studied at the Royal Swedish Academy of Arts and in 1904 he illustrated his first book, 'Lappland'. He is best known for his illustrations in early editions of 'Bland tomtar och troll' (Among Gnomes and Trolls), featuring stories of Swedish folklore and fairy tales.

Bauer's troll illustrations were of a grotesque style but with a touch of humour, appealing to both children and adults alike. Most of his works are watercolours usually in muted colours over pen and ink line work.

This enchanting compilation features 83 of Bauer's best works mostly from various editions of 'Bland tomtar och troll'. This superb collection is certain to delight lovers of fairy tale illustration and also Bauer admirers.

SA

Compiled and edited by Steve Archibald

Copyright © 2018 Redcrest Publishing

All rights reserved


ISBN: 978-1-9996677-0-2


Redcrest Publishing
9 Chalfont Close, Hemel Hempstead, Herts. HP2 7JR


Front Cover: Illustration from 'The Changelings'
Back Cover: Illustration from 'The Golden Key'

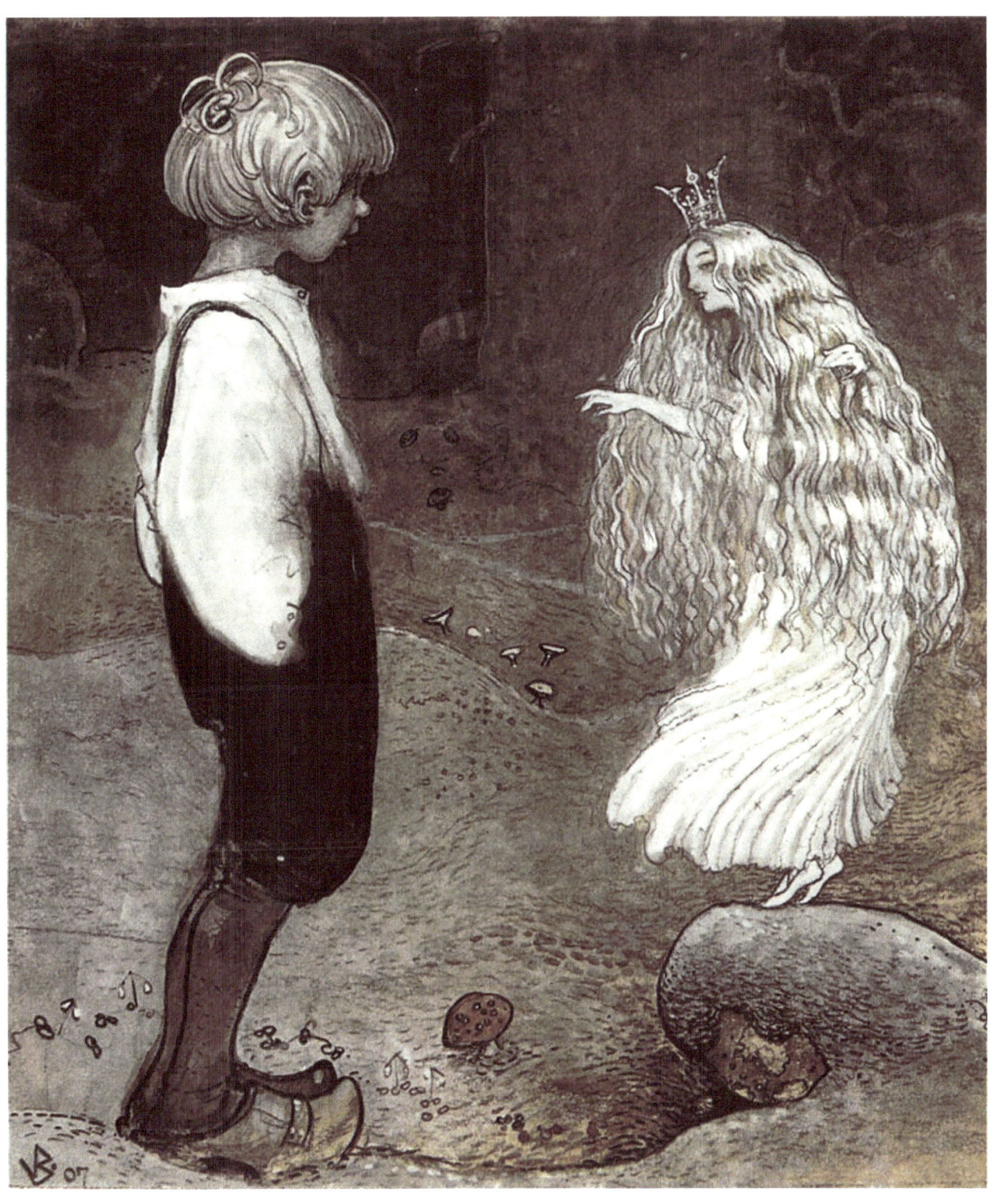

At that moment the frog became a beautiful fairy girl.
From 'The Seven Wishes'

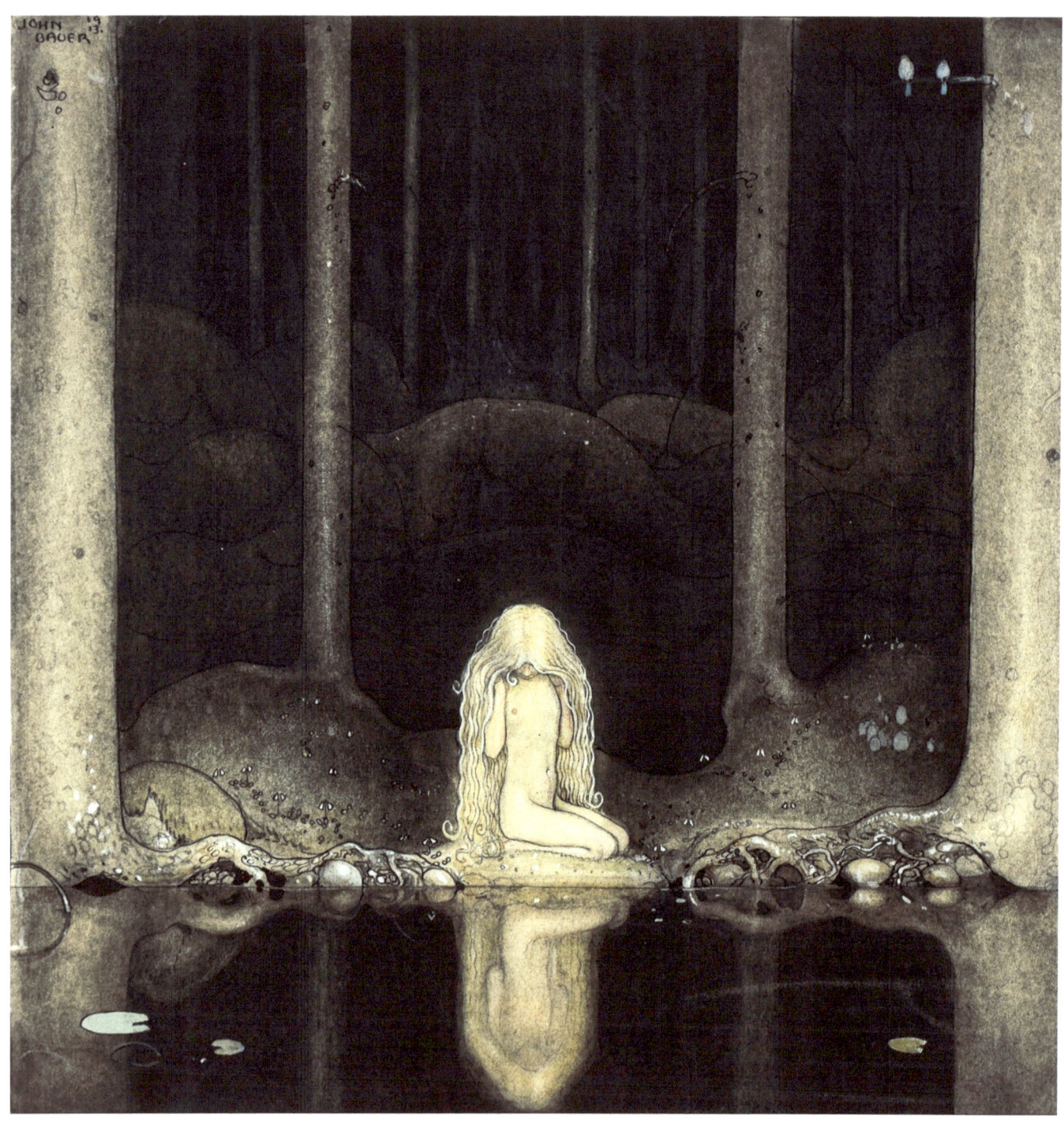

Princess Tuvstarr gazing down into the dark waters of the forest tarn

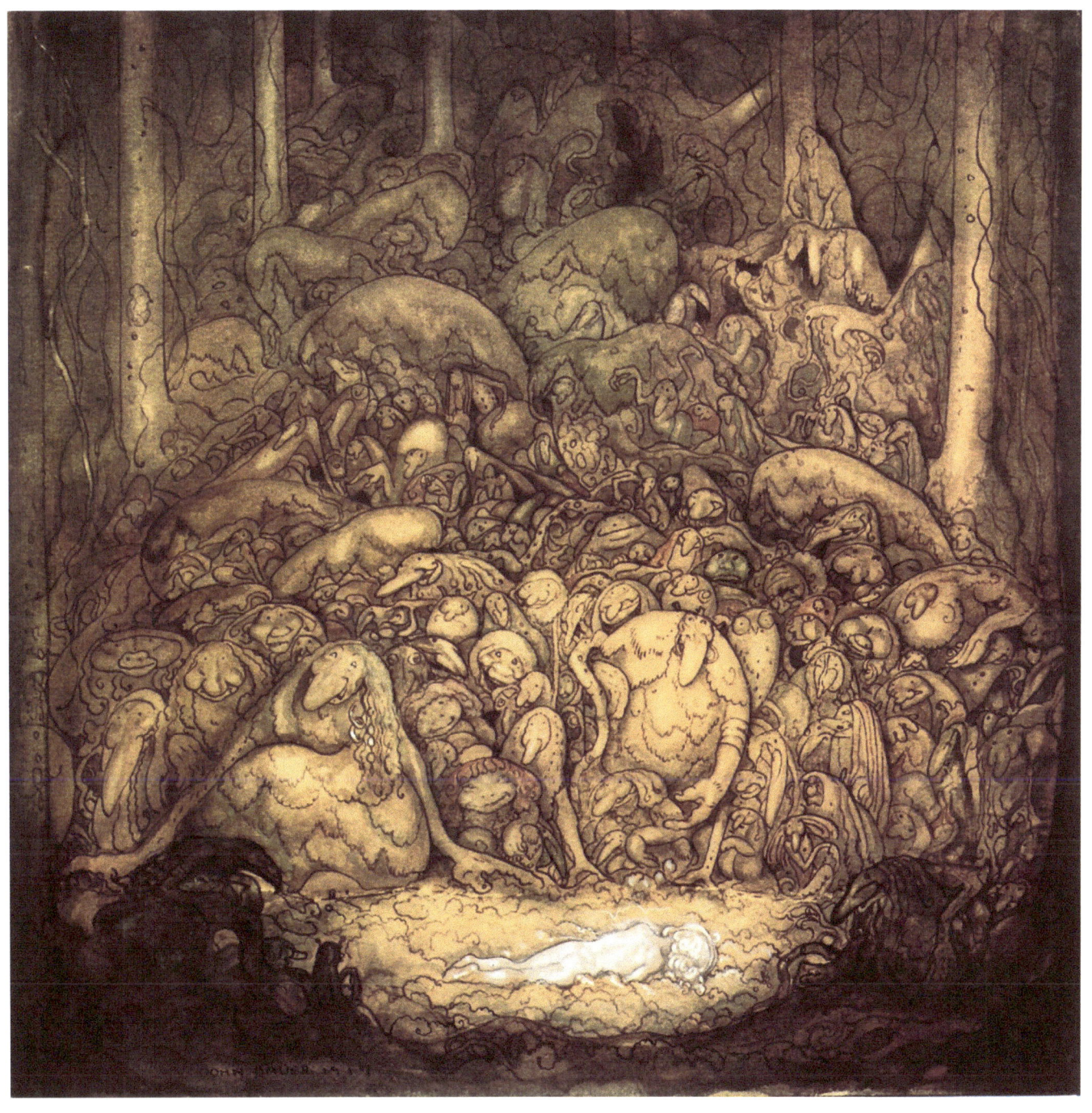

Root Trolls

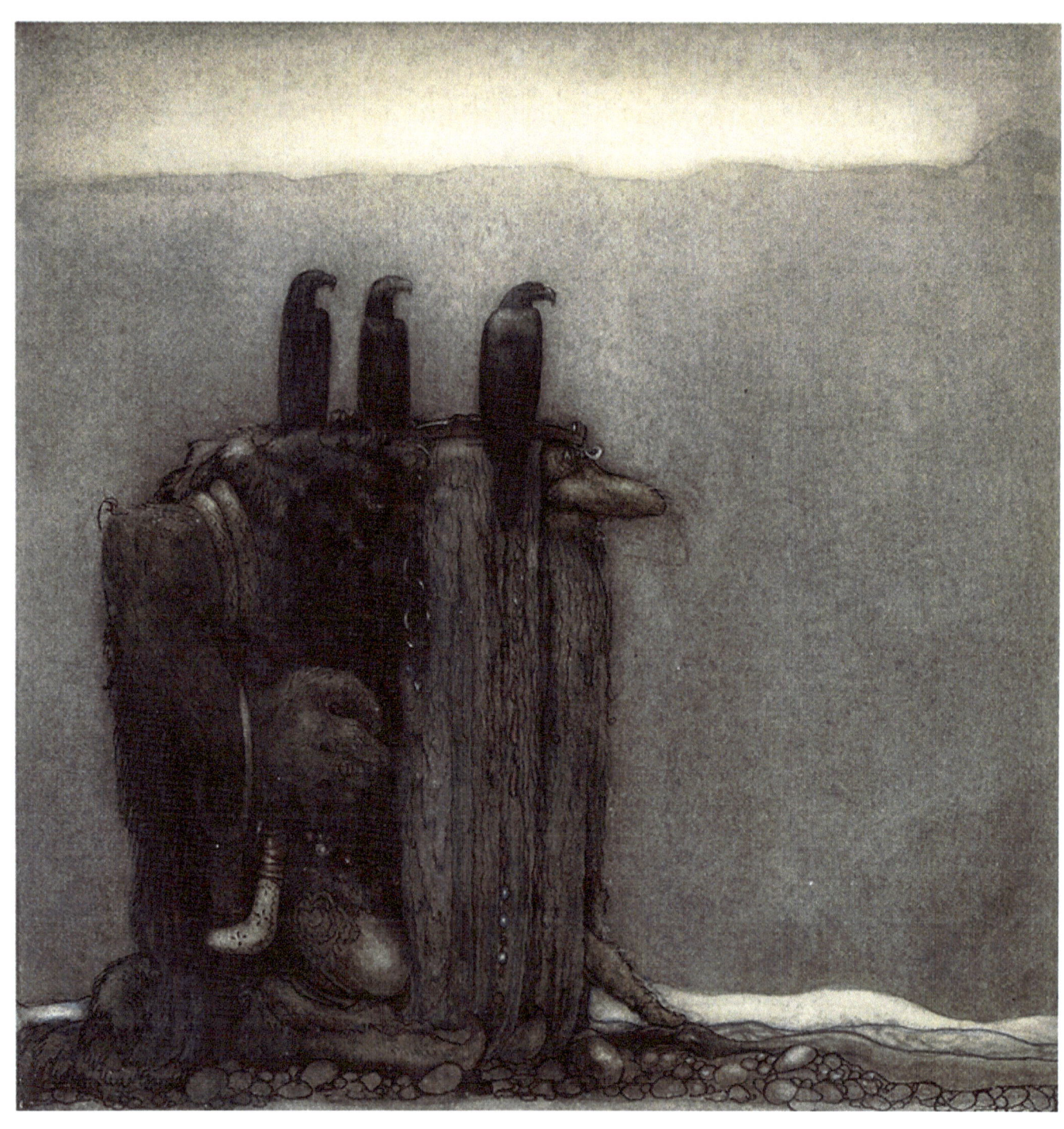

Mountain Troll

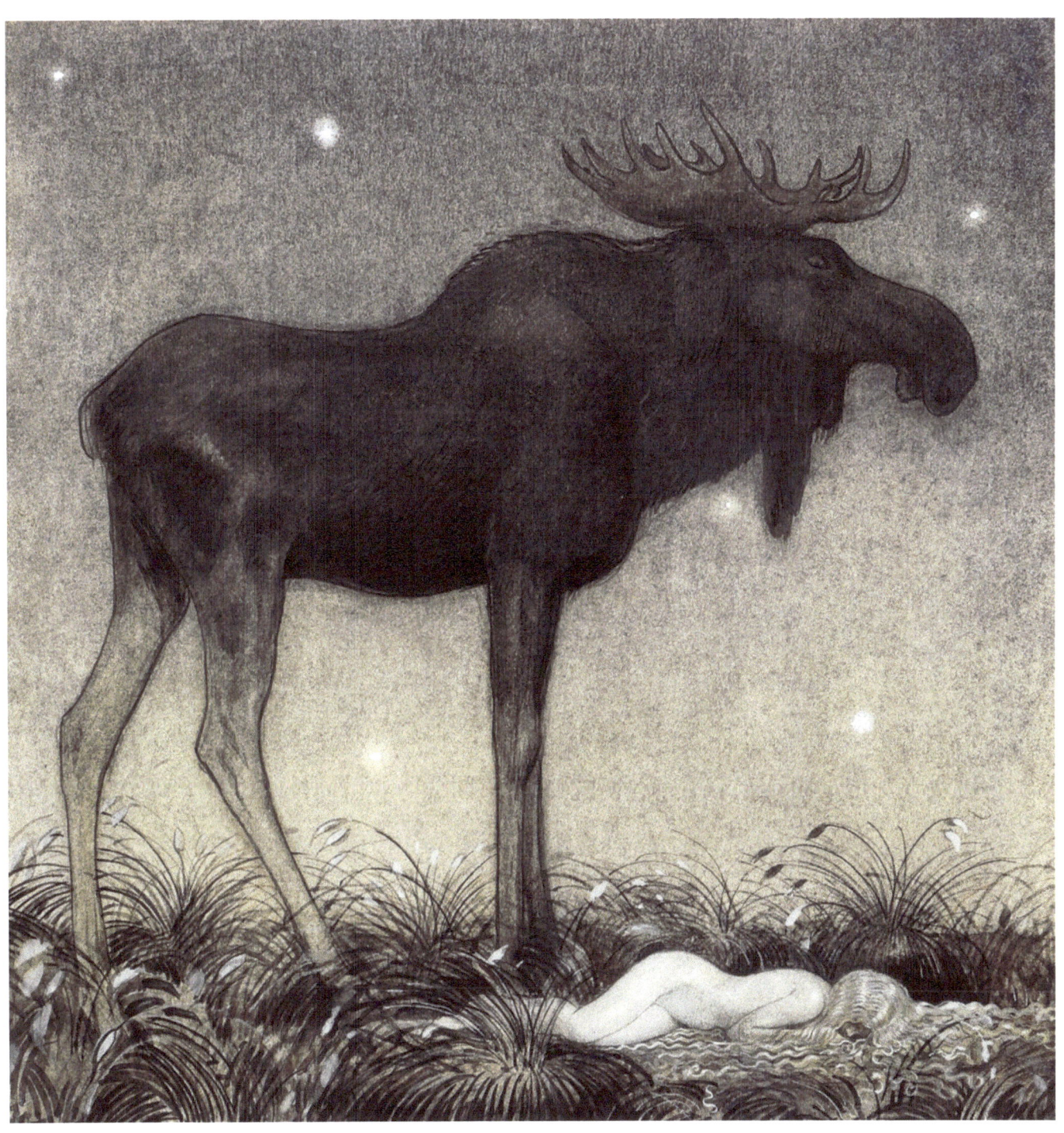

Leap the Elk and the Little Princess Cottongrass

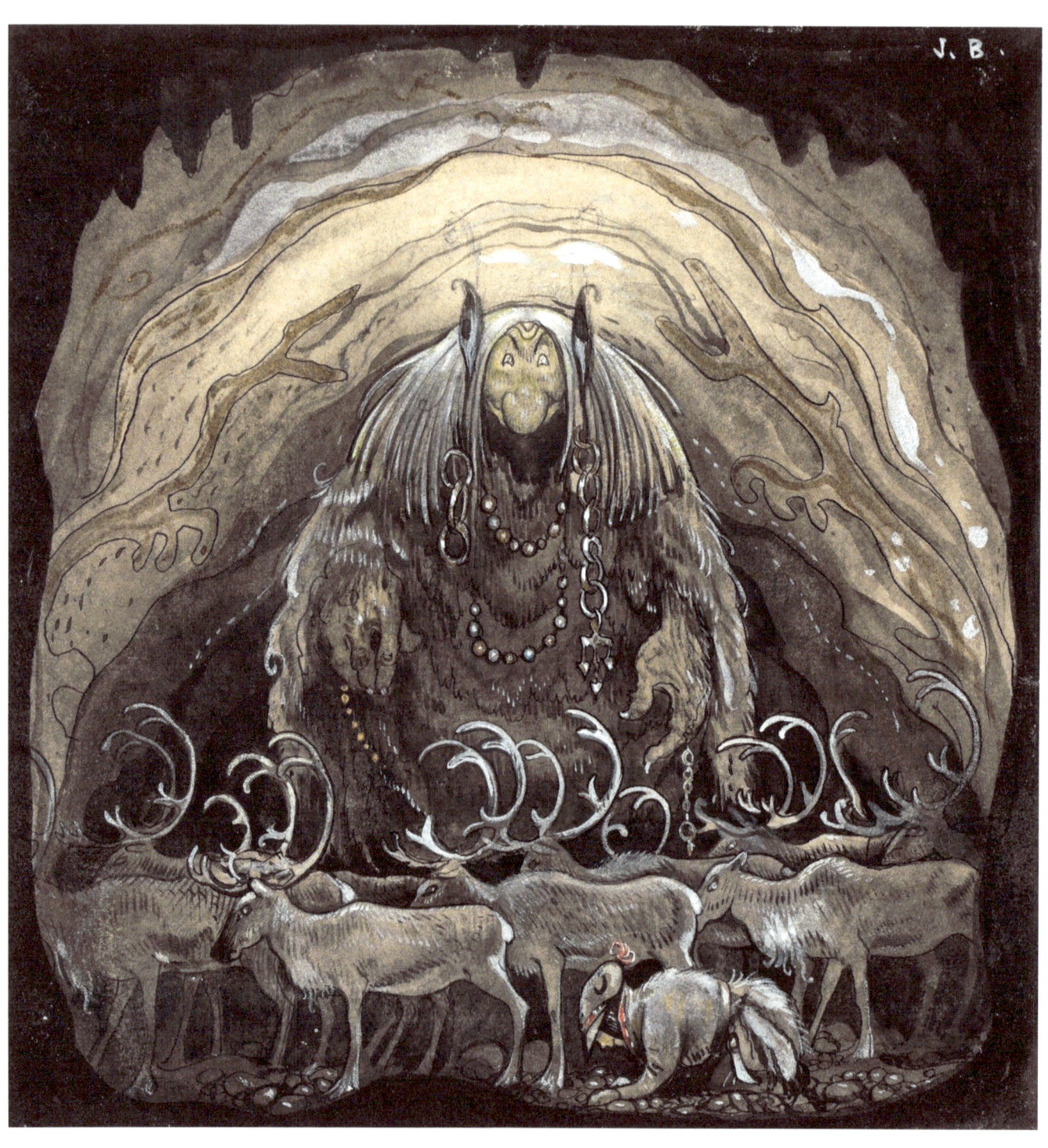

Nila's Victim, The Christmas Book ( Nila's offer ).

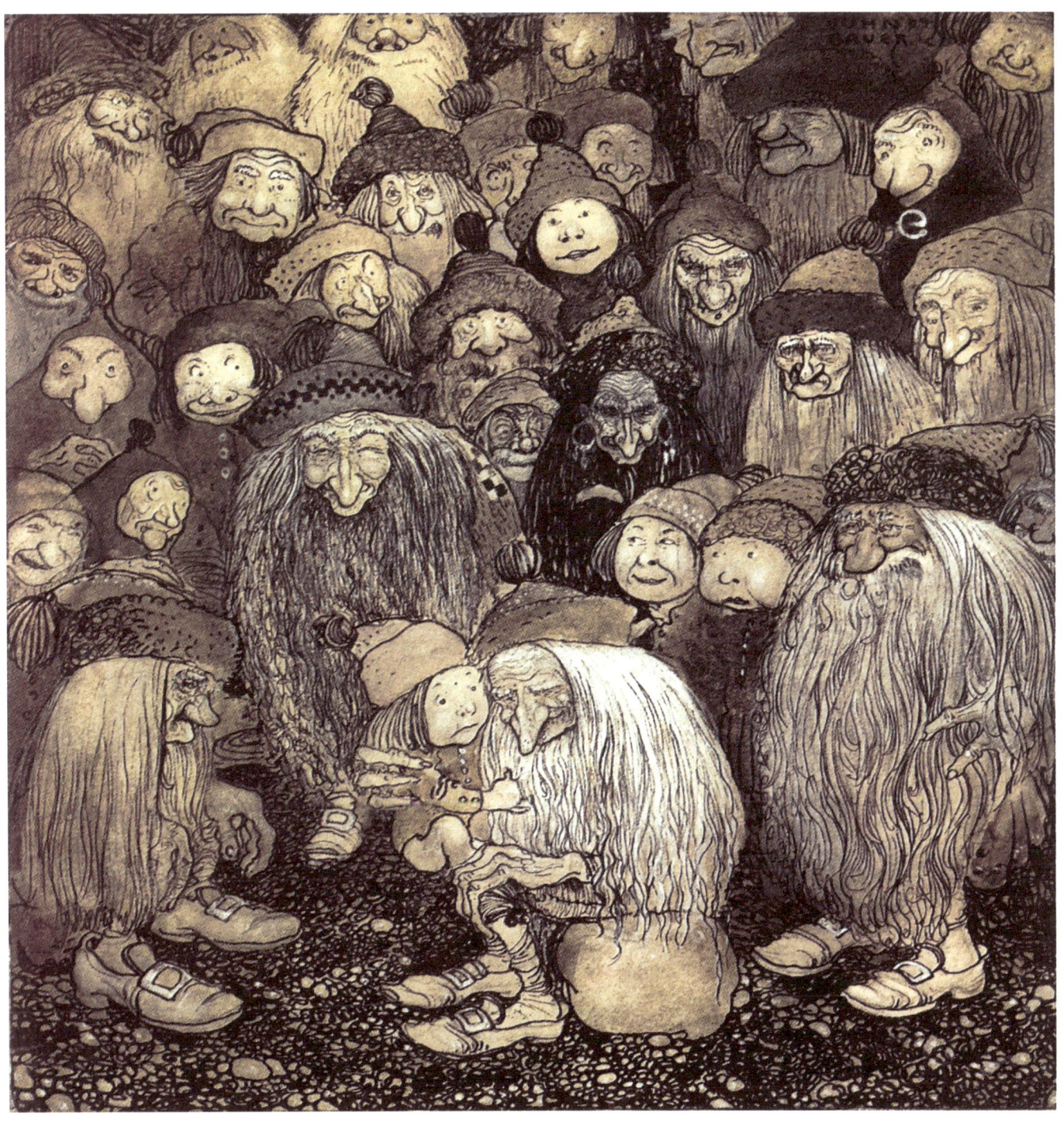

'"But how do I get into the mountain" the gnome boy asked.
From 'The Trolls and the Youngest Tomte'

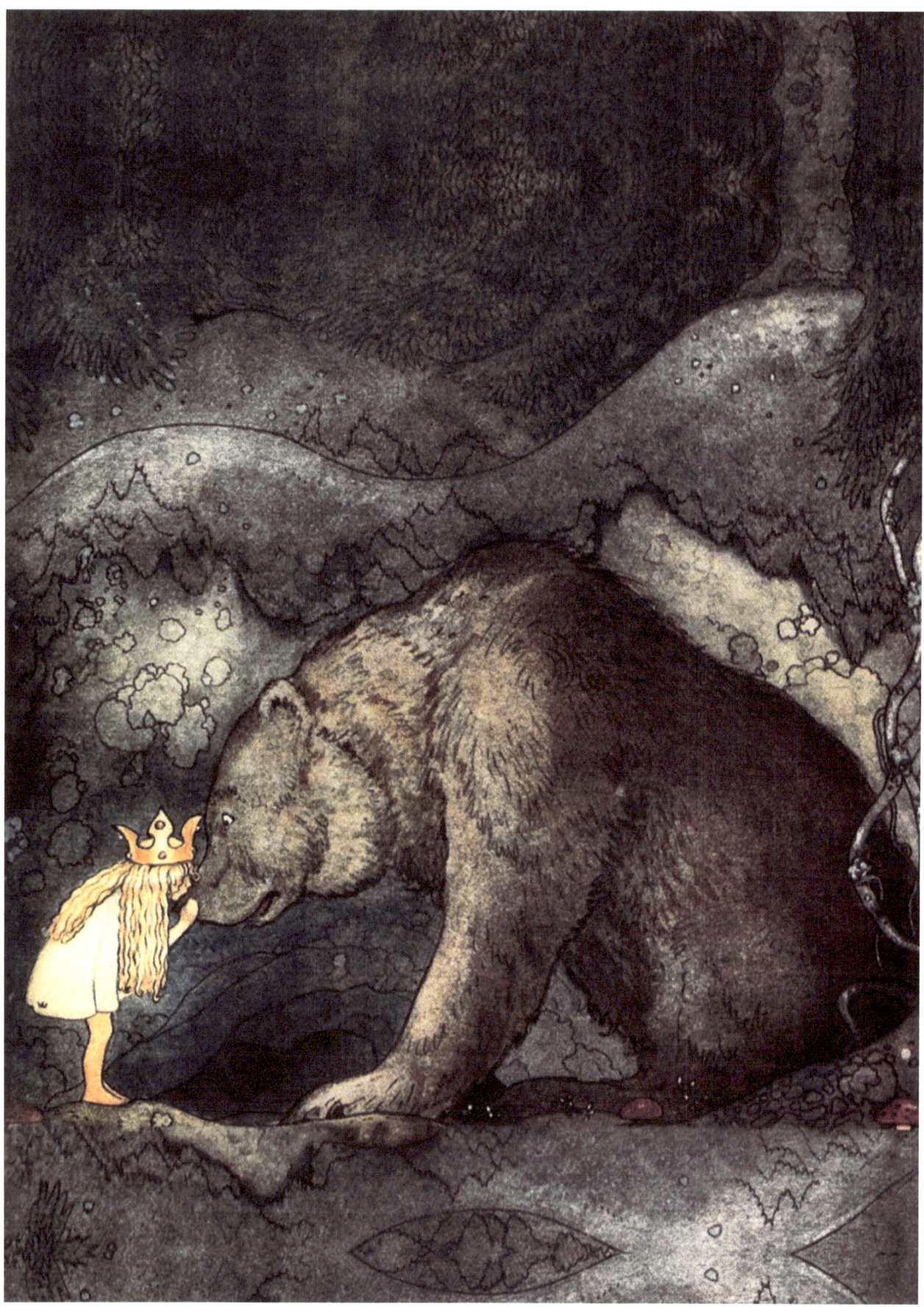

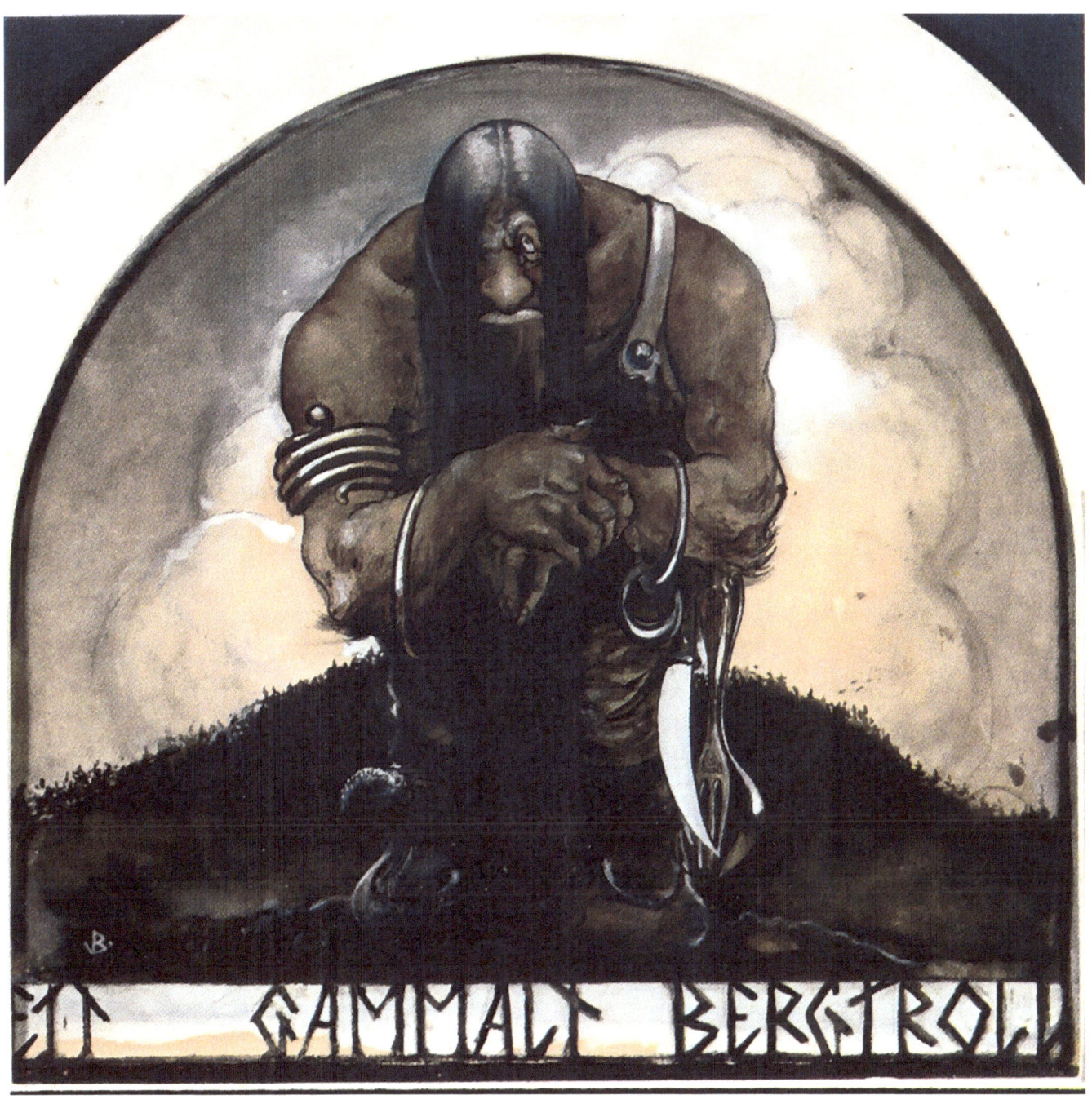

Above: An old mountain troll.

Left: She Kissed the Bear on the Nose.
From 'Innocence Hiking'

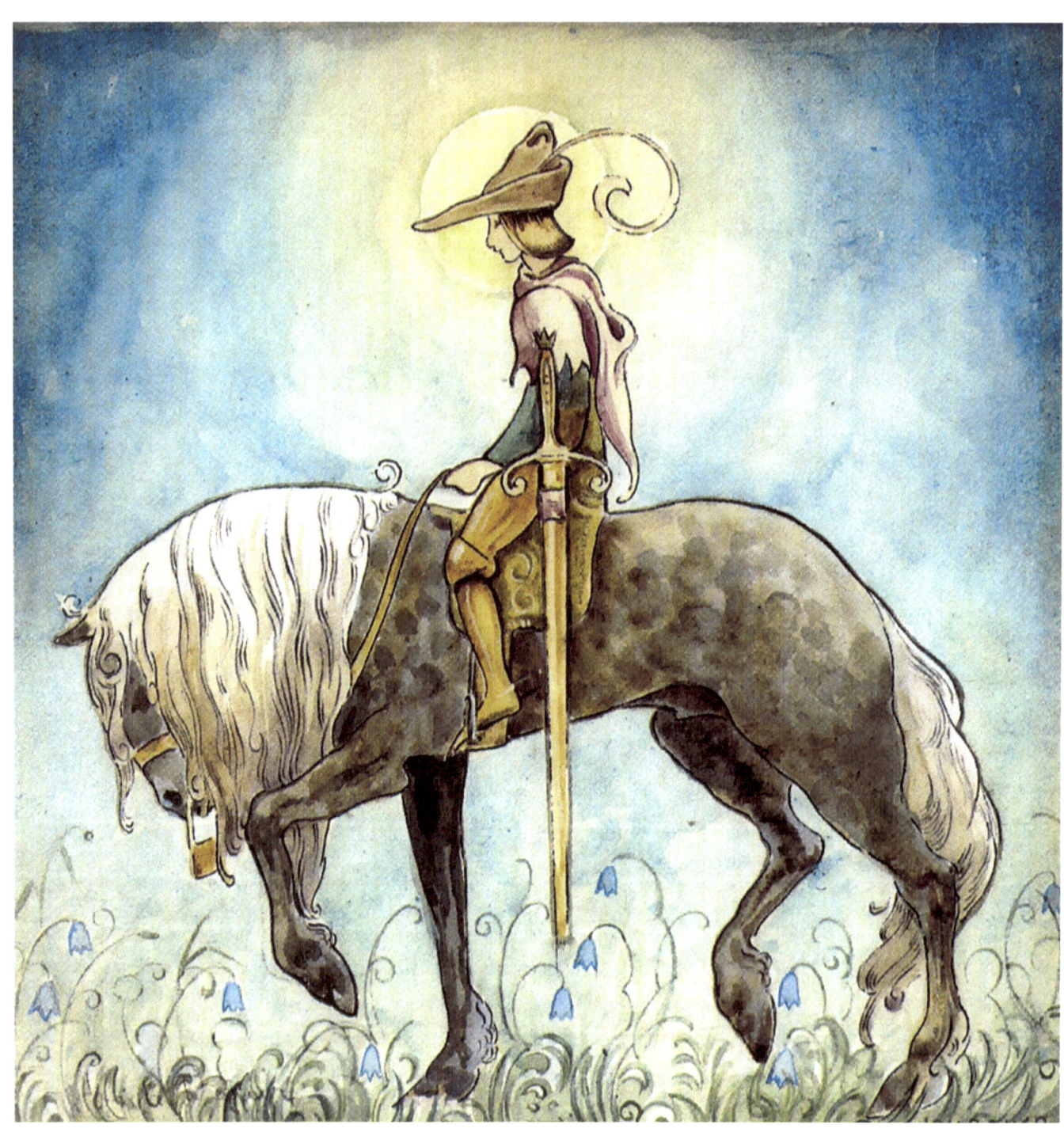

From 'The Magic Ride'

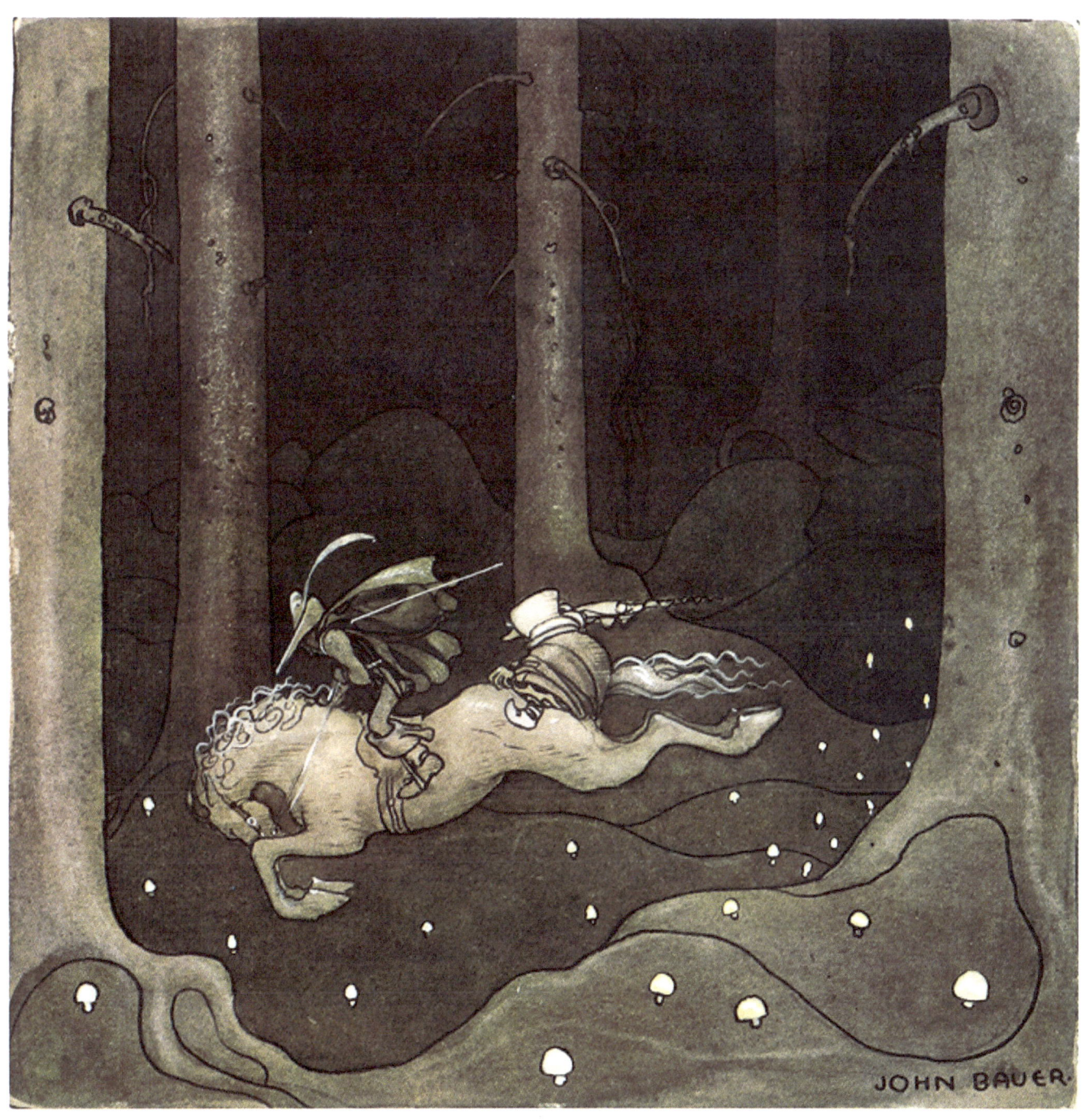

From 'The Magic Ride'

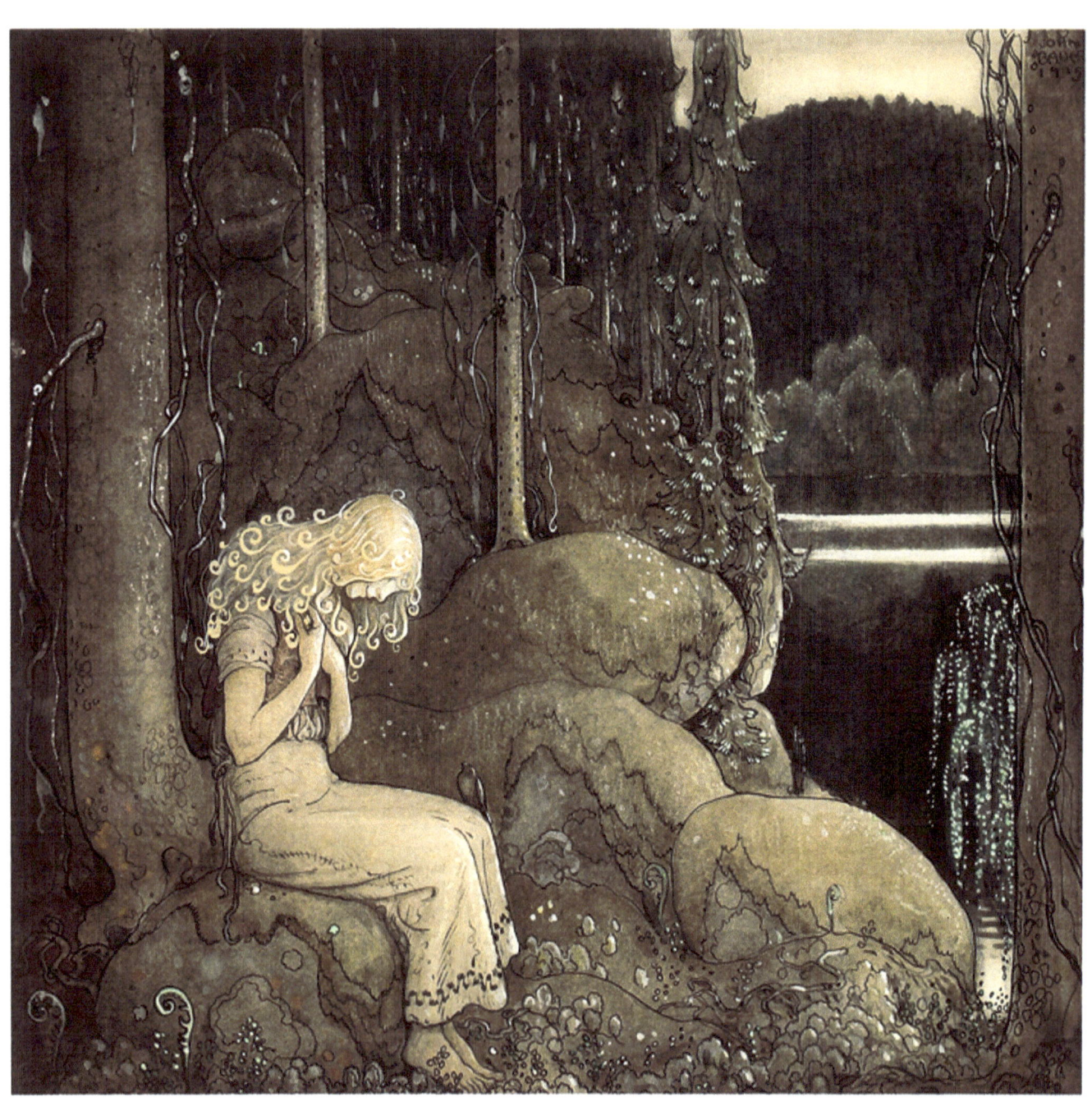

She rested beside the lake.
From 'A Knight Rode Forth'.

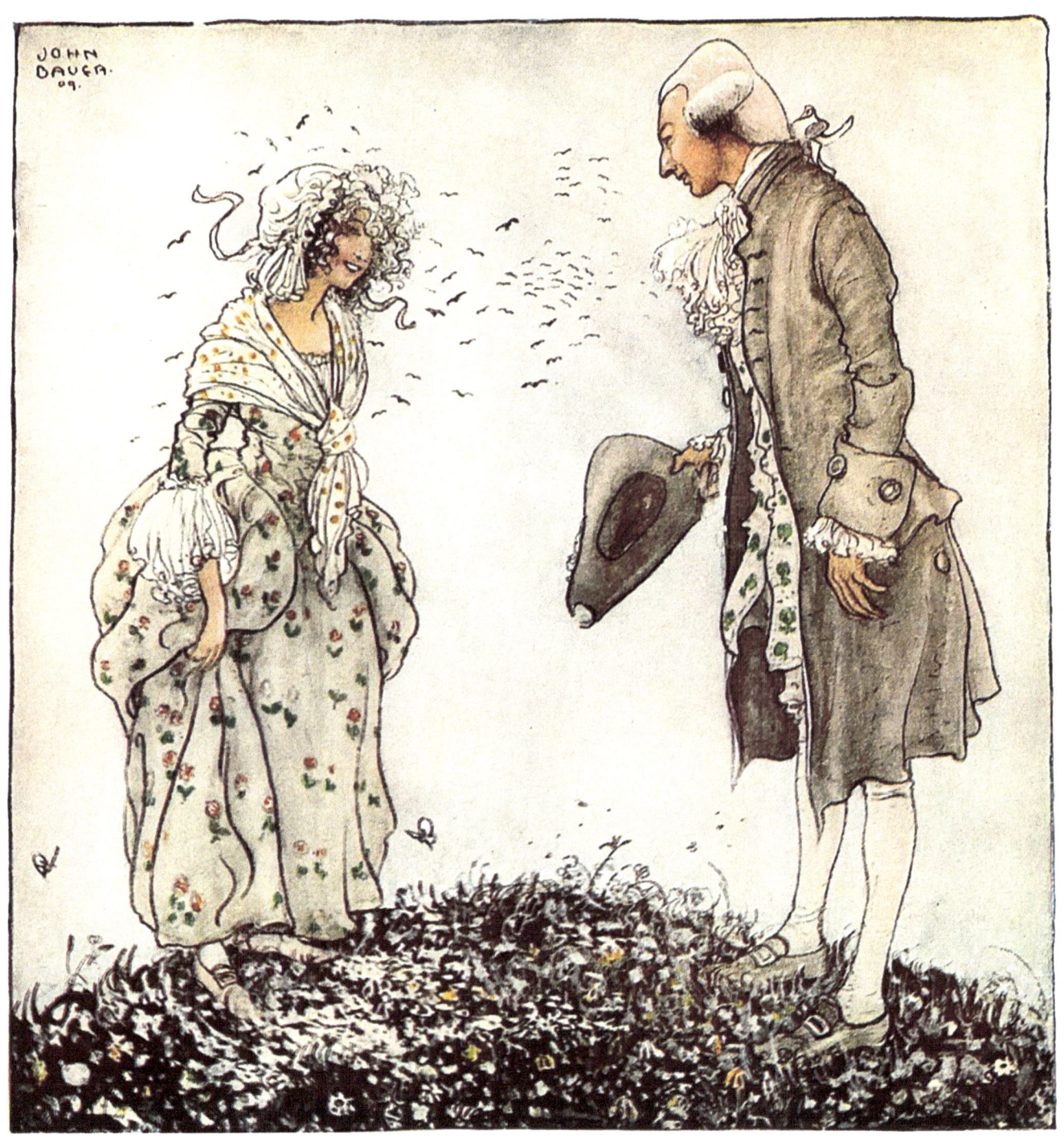

Cinderella

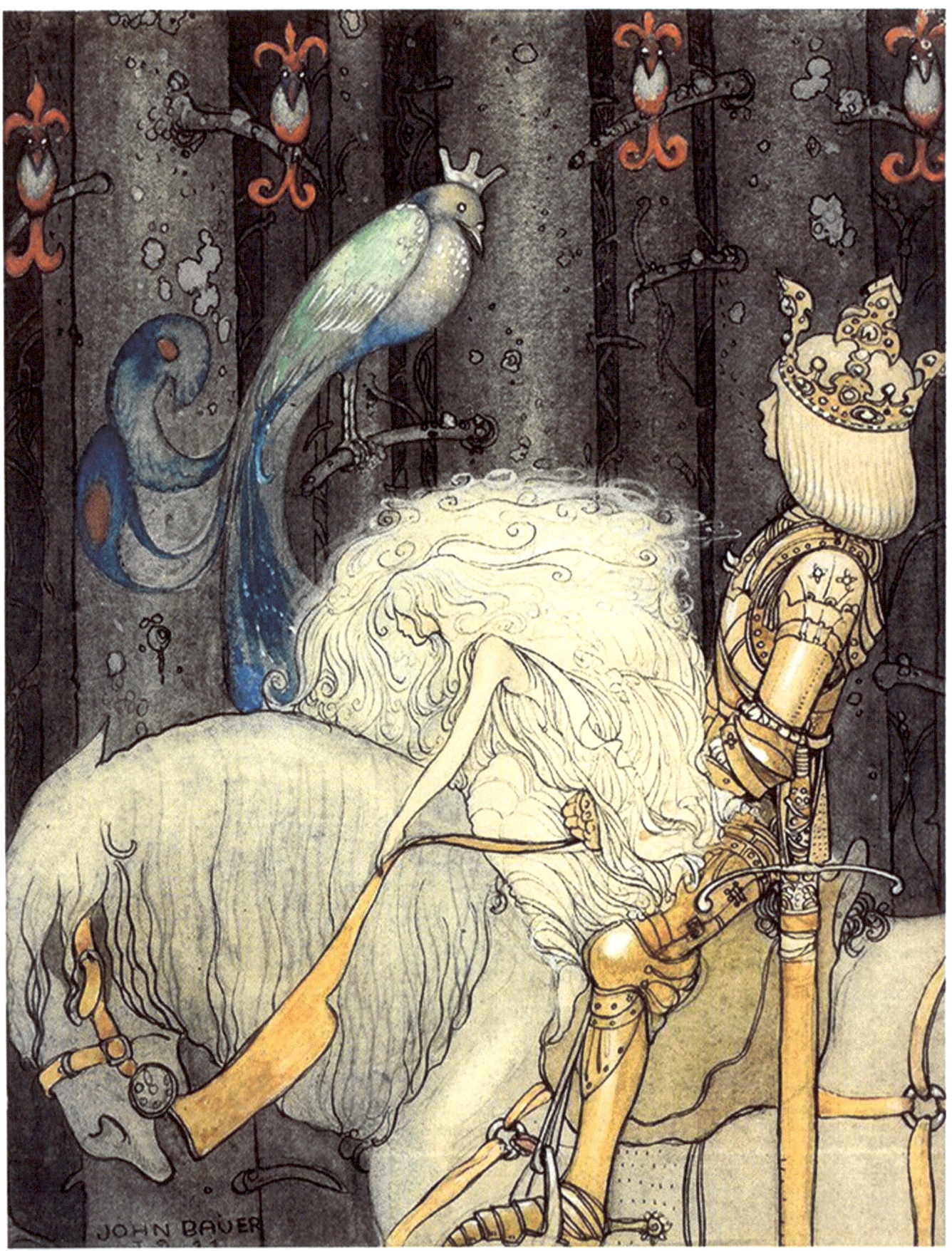

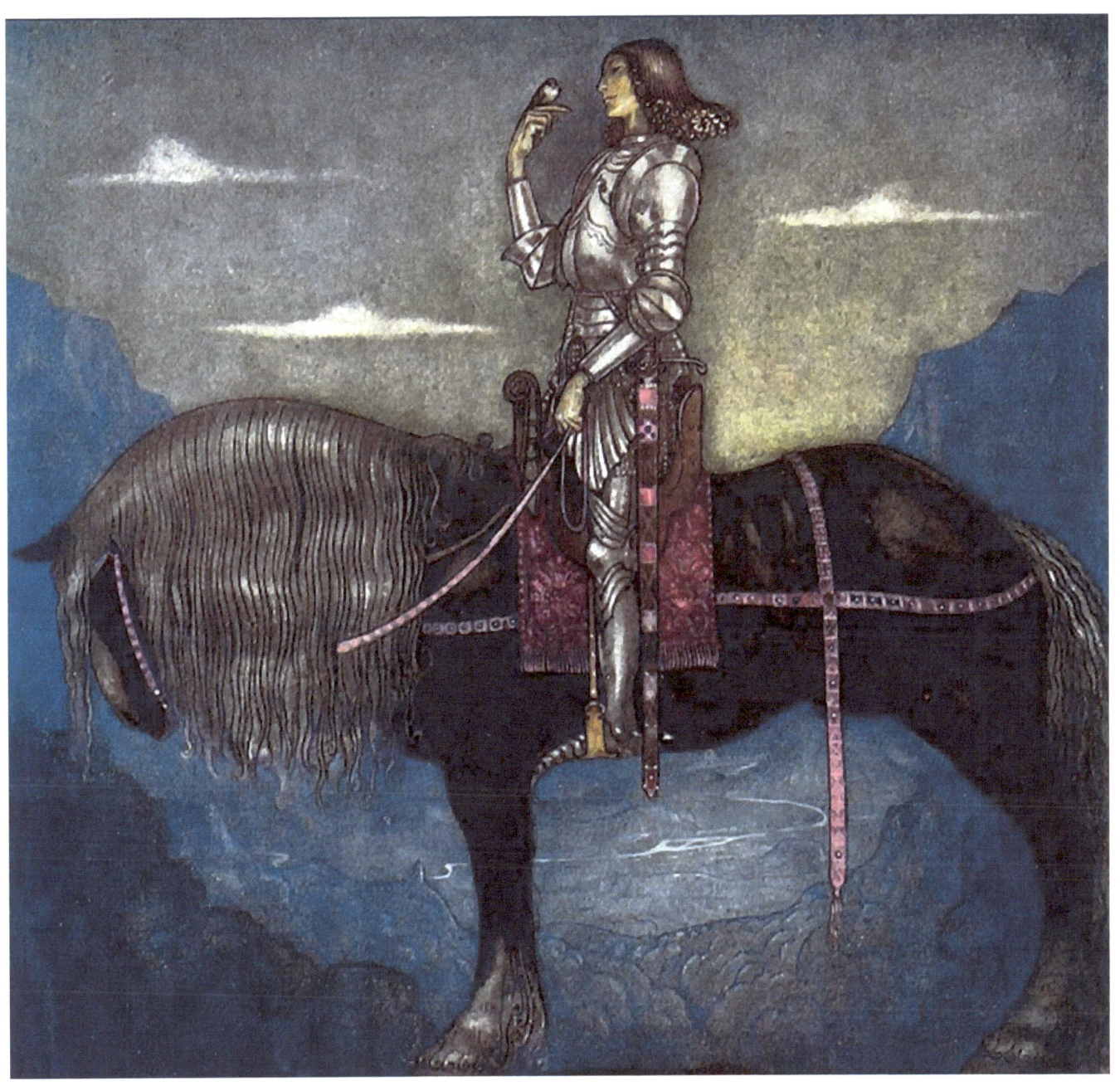

Above: I come with one hundred greetings from one, which you did well receive, said the sparrow. From 'A Knight Rode Forth'.

Left: Blue Bird.

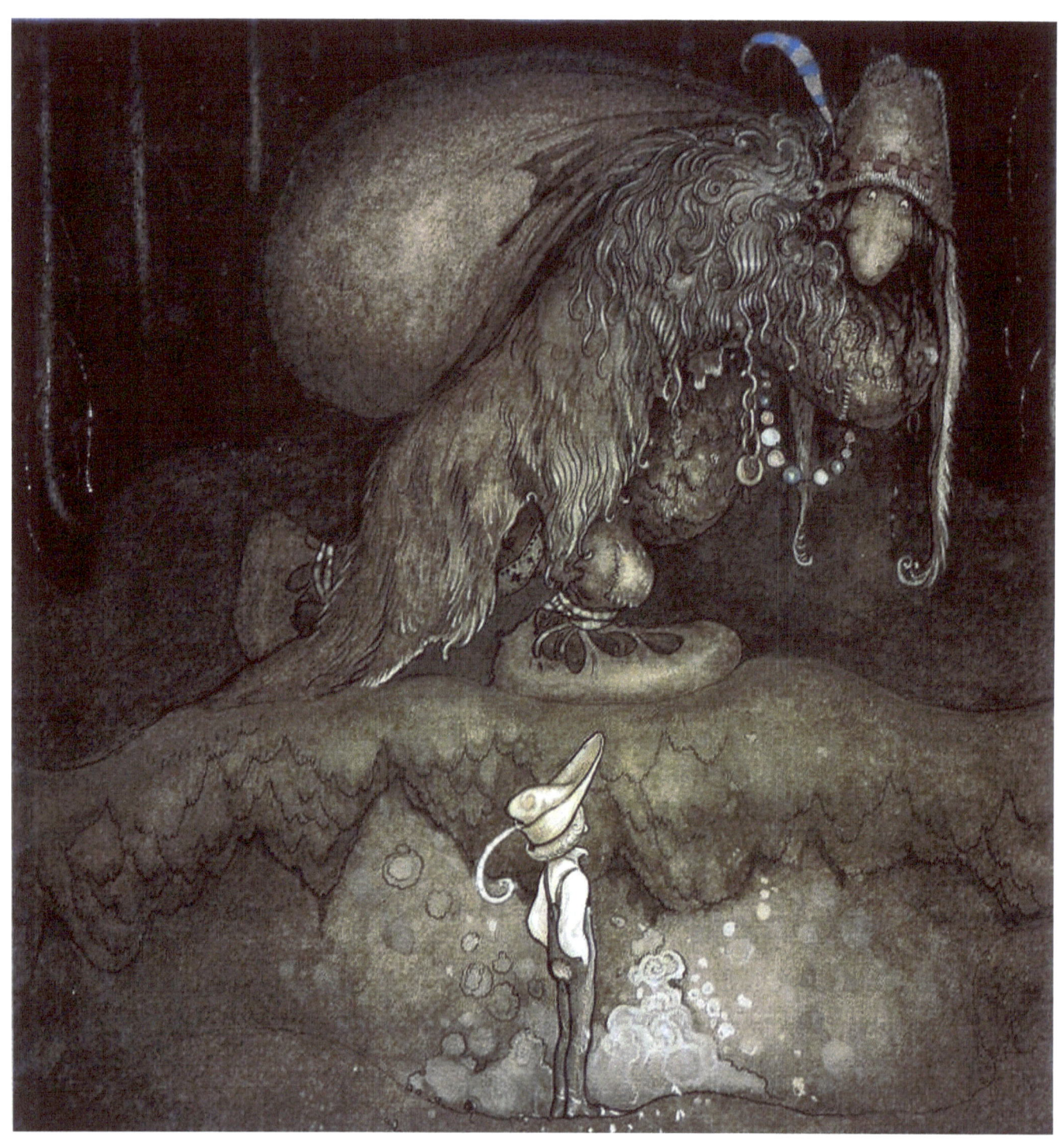

Good evening uncle! greeted the boy.
From 'The Boy and the Trolls'

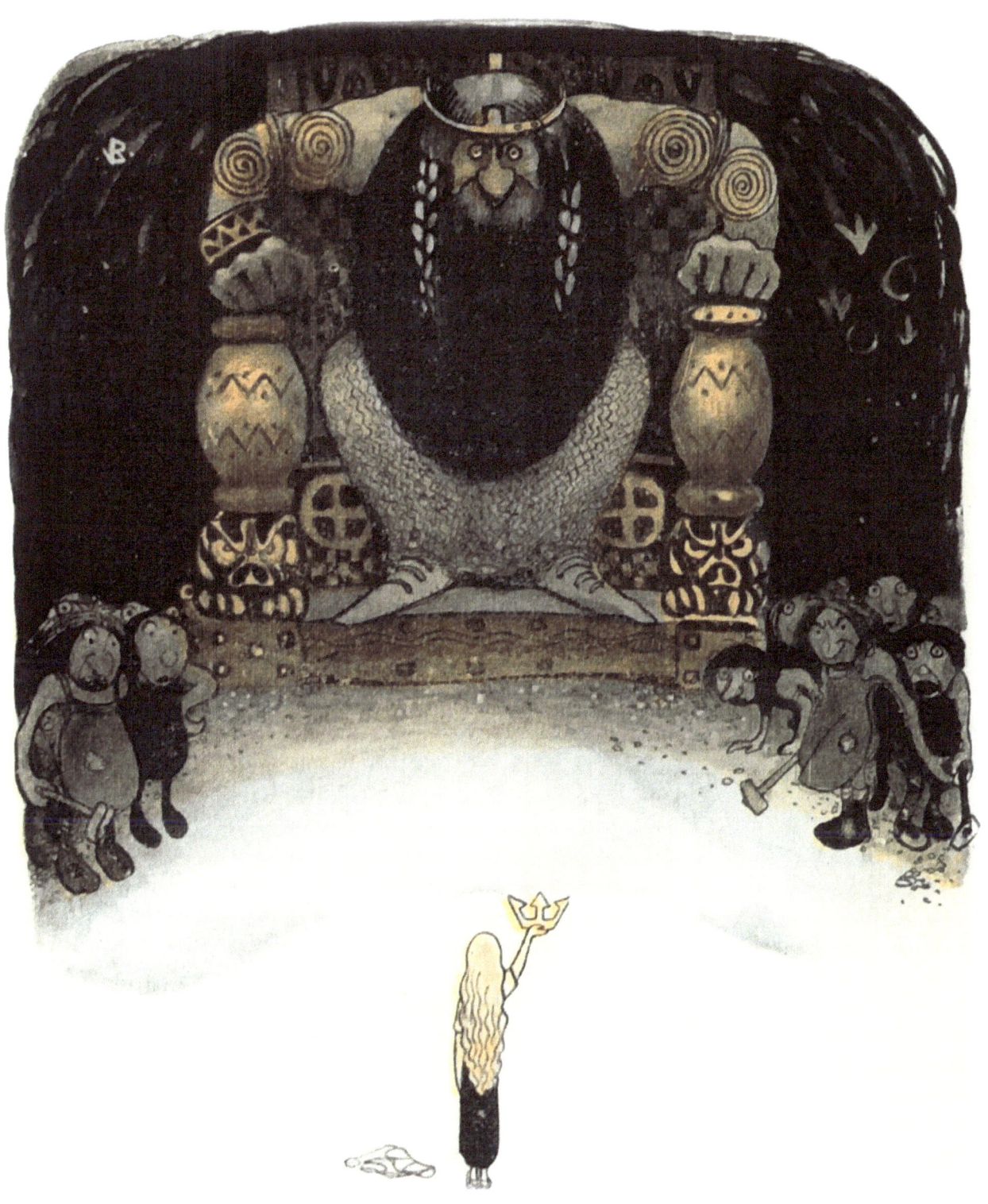

"I have the crown."
From 'Dag and Daga, and the Flying Troll of Sky Mountain'

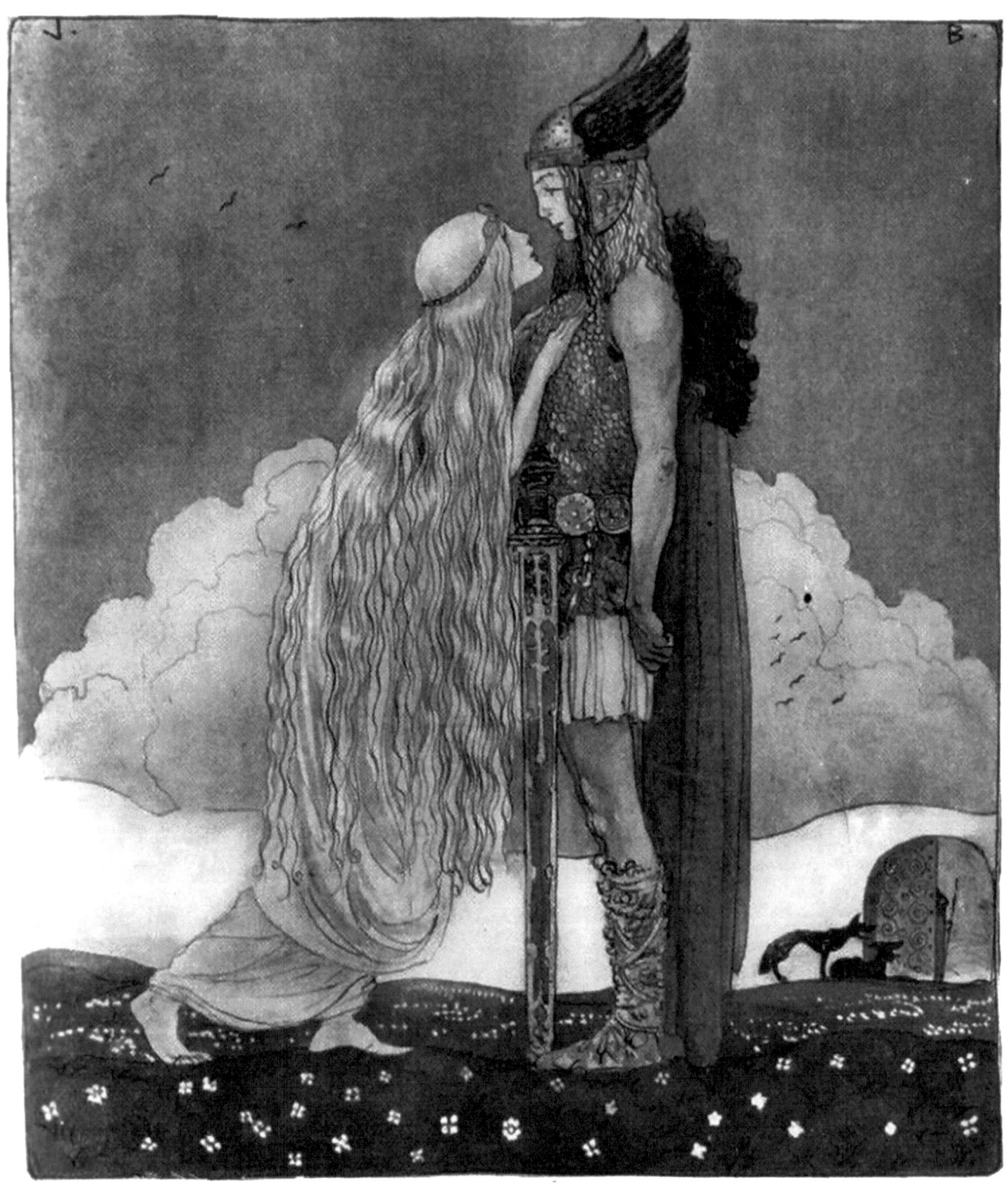

Freyja Greets Svipdag.
From 'Godsaga'

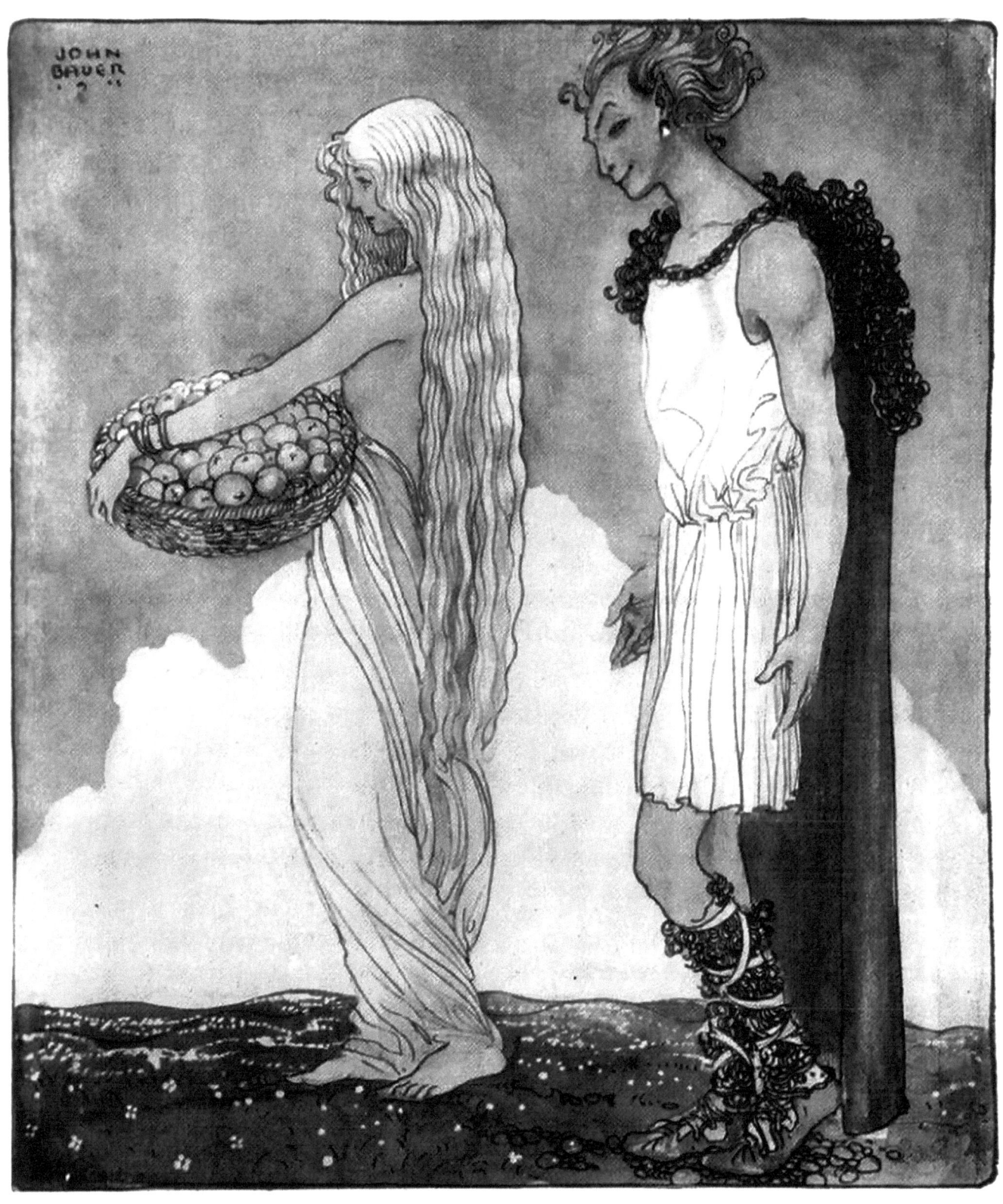

Loki and Idun.
From 'Godsaga'

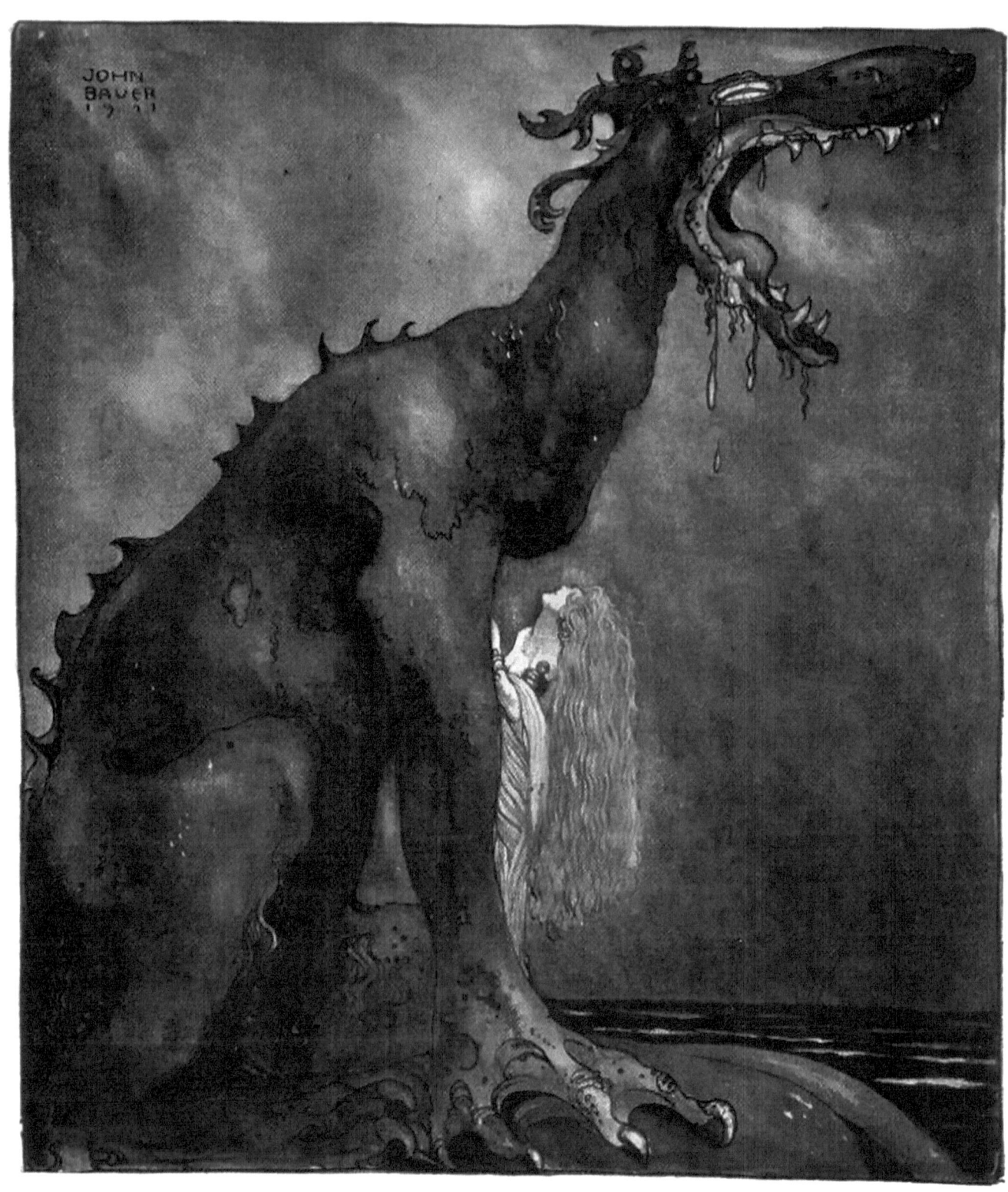

Svipdag transformed.
From 'Godsaga'

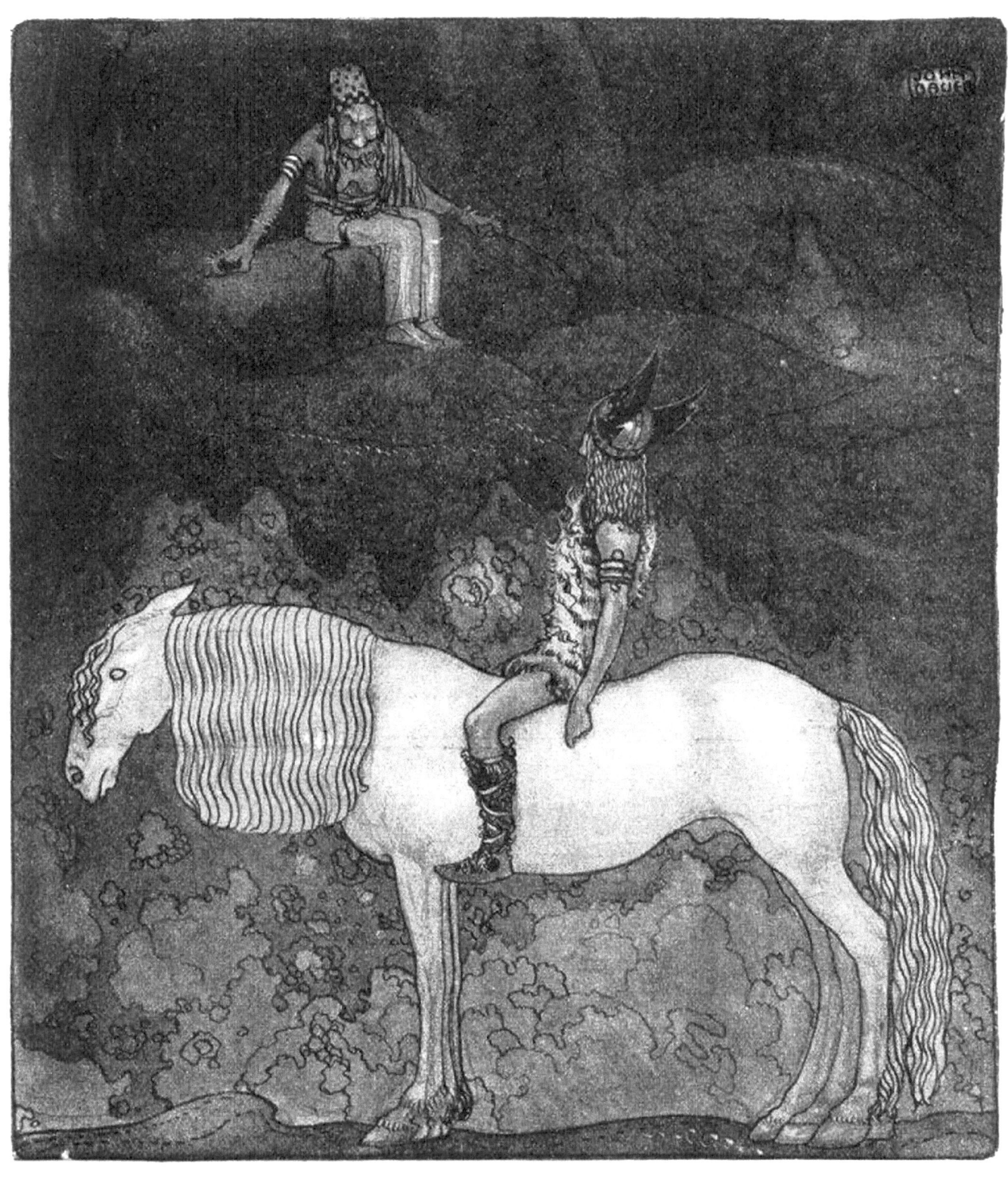

Svipdag speaks with Thokk.
From 'Godsaga'

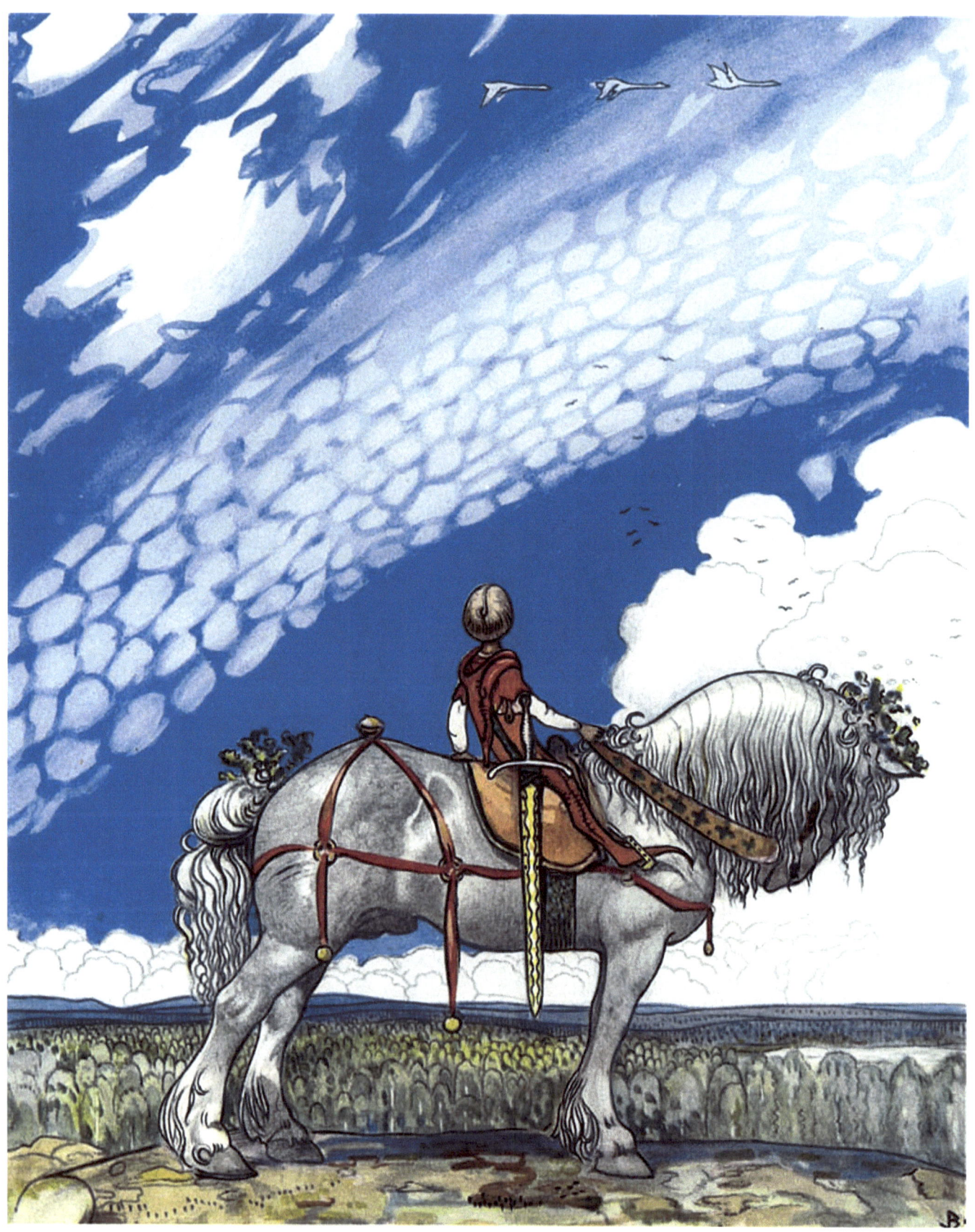

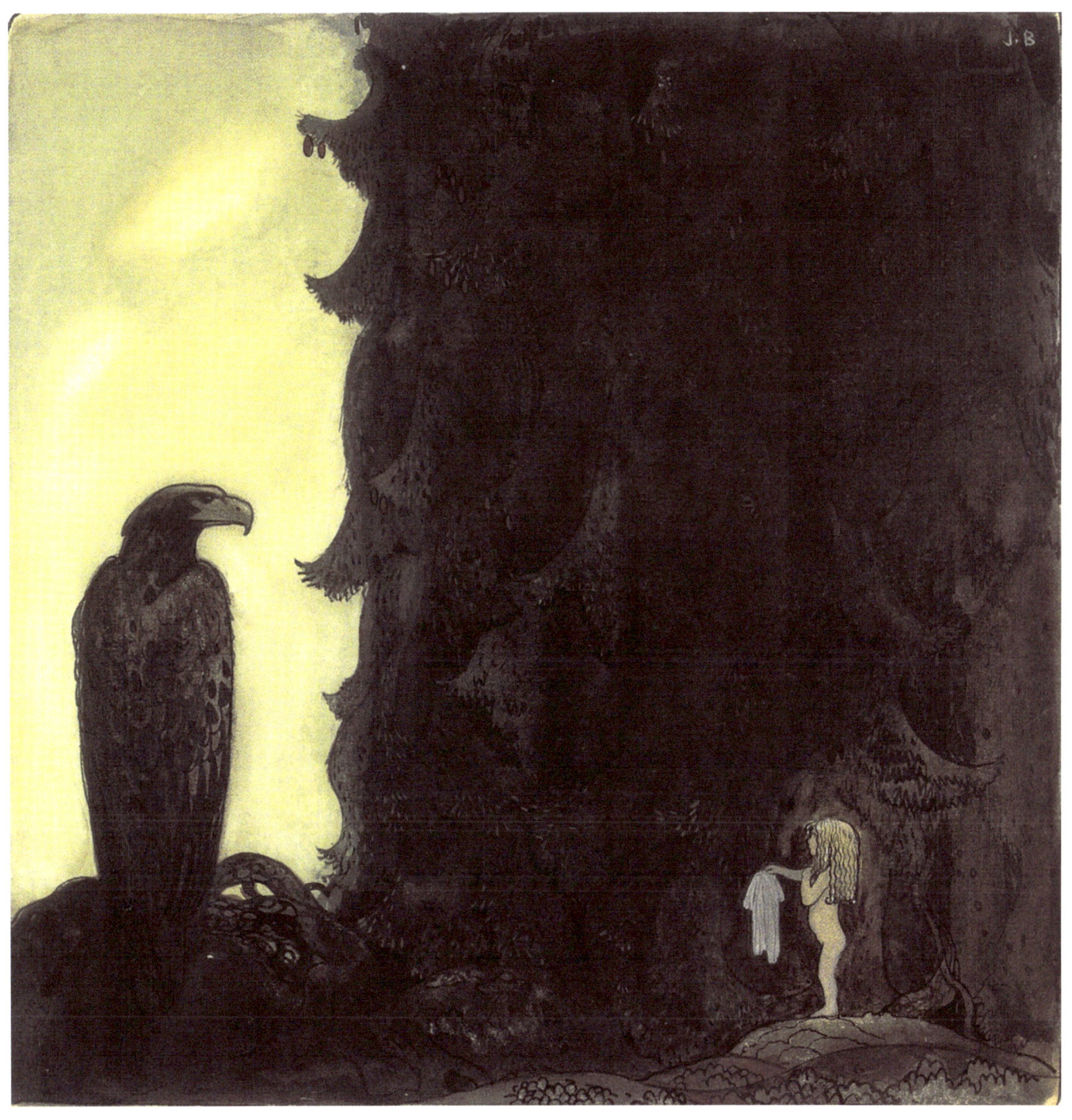

Above: "Here are the rest of my clothes."
From 'Innocence Hiking'

Left: Into the Wide World.

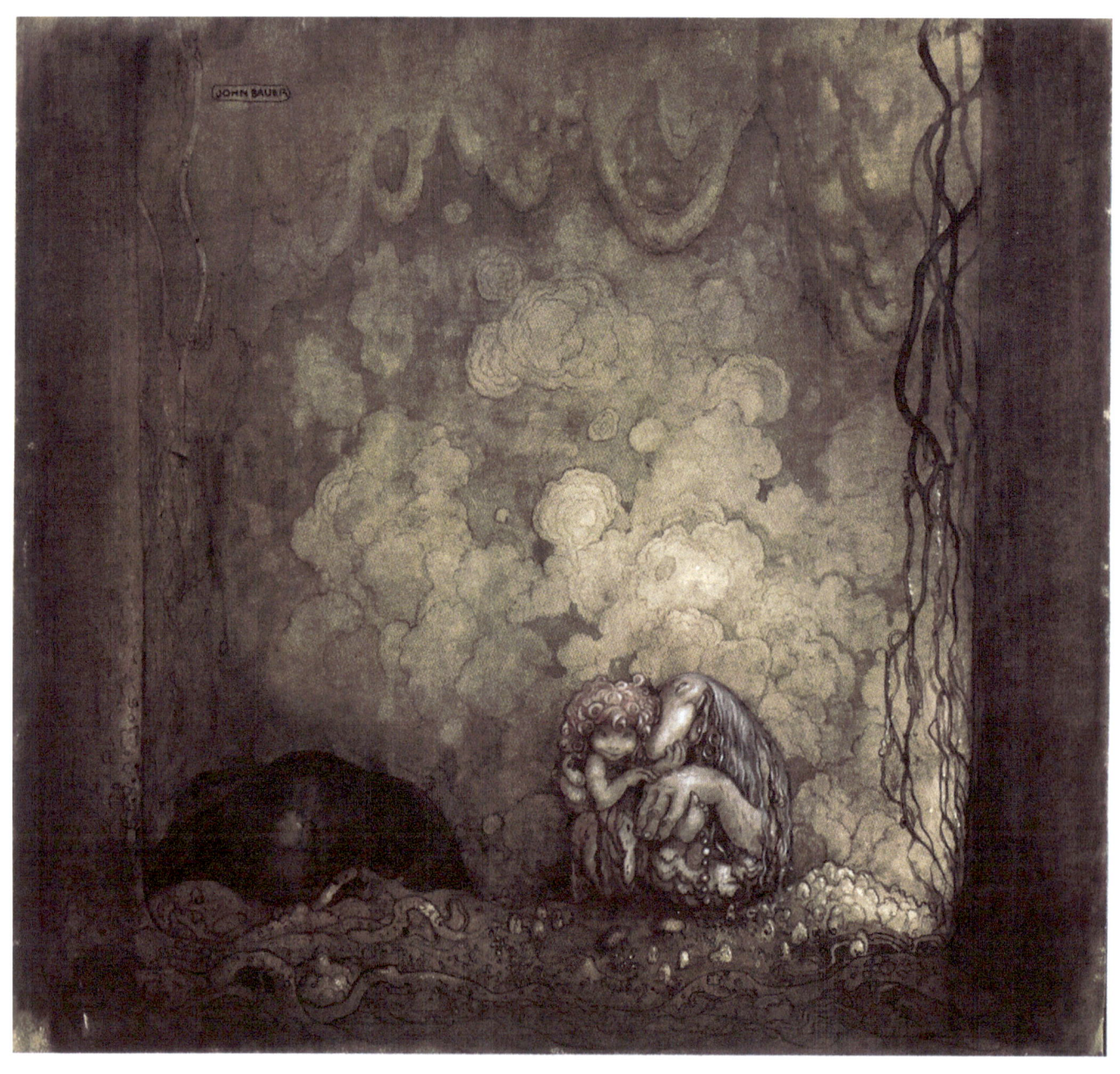

Above: Humpe

Right: Julebocken, Yule Goat.
From 'A Polar Bear's Tale'

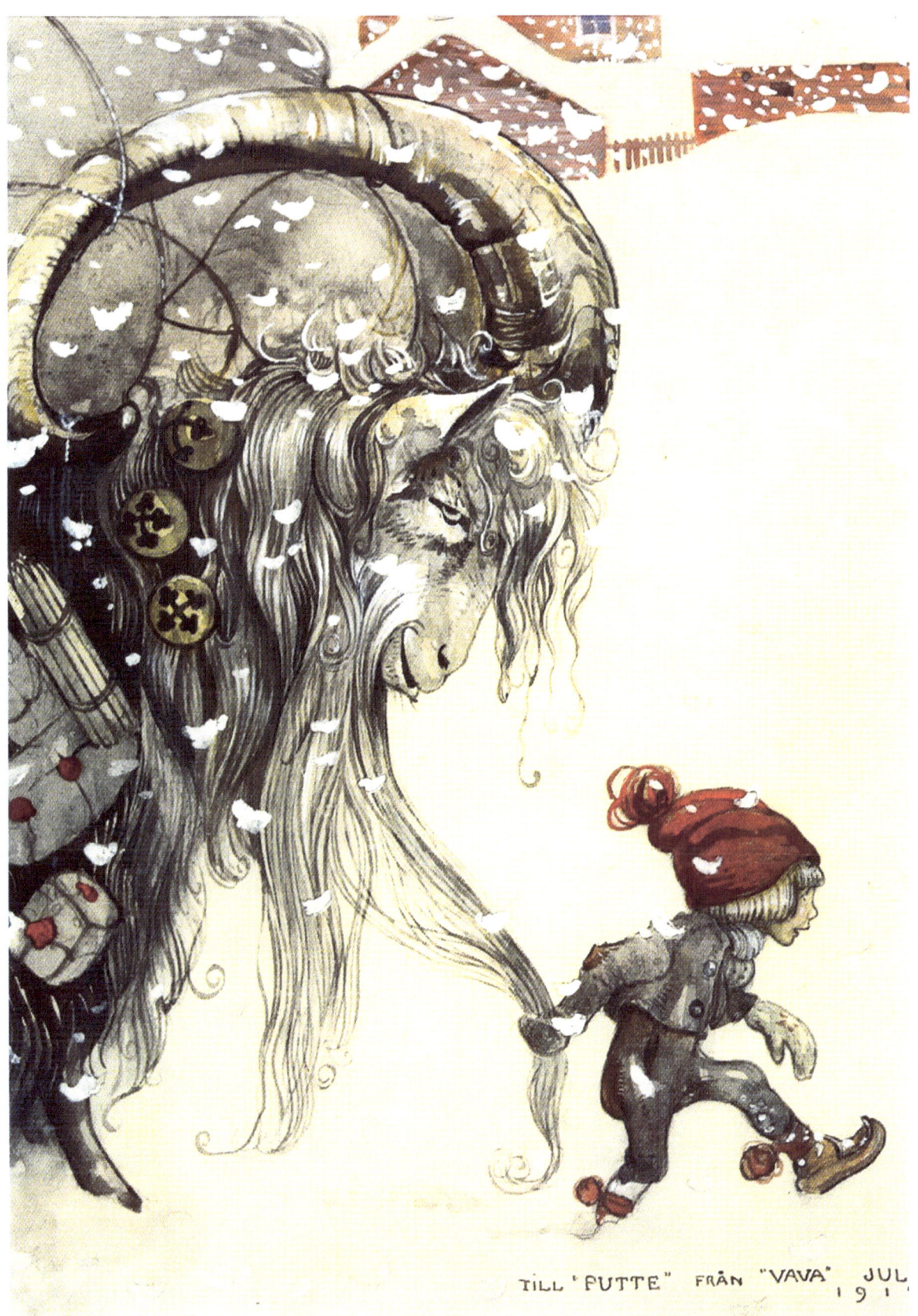

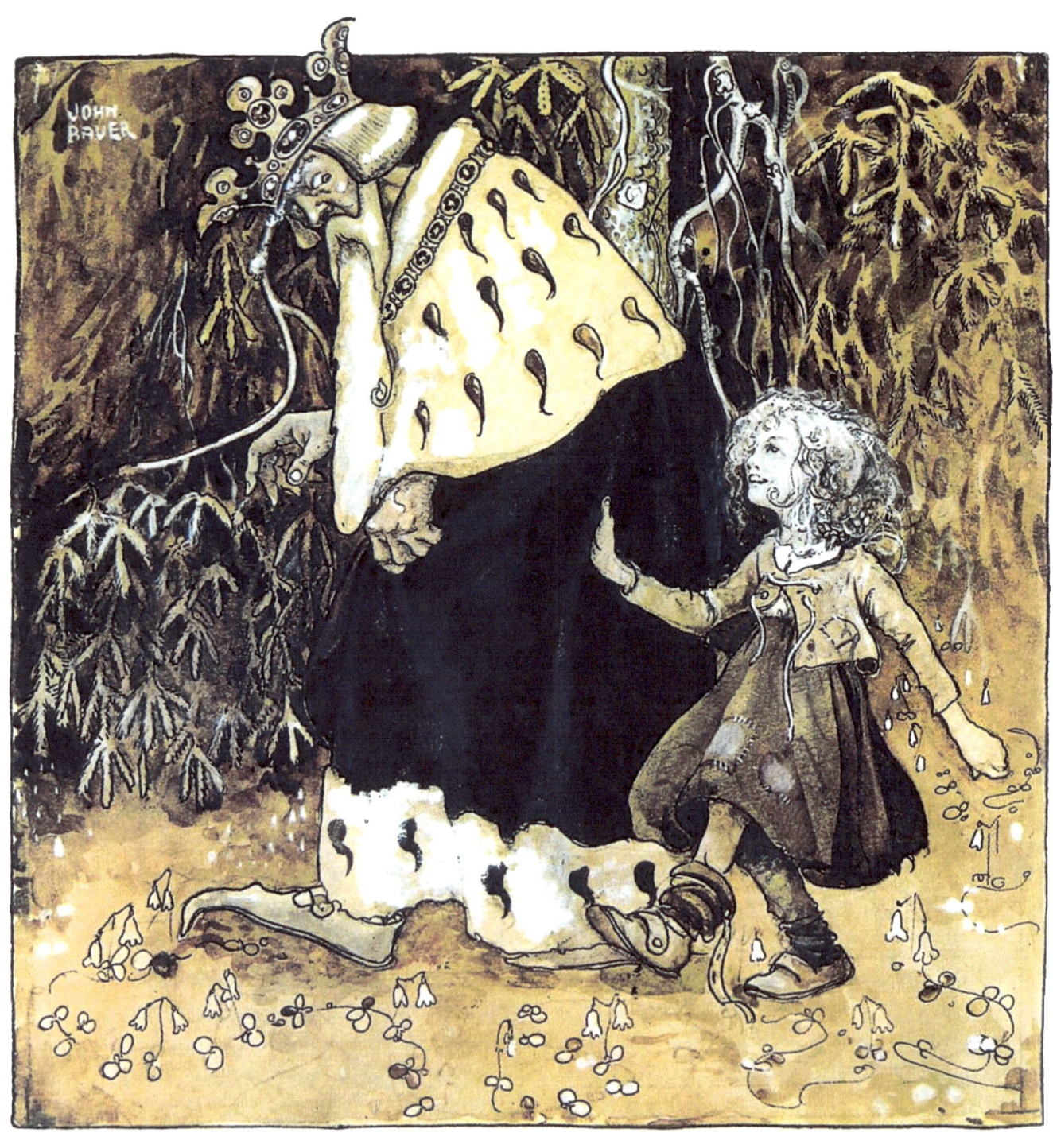

Above: Linda Gull and the Old King.

Right: Little Boy Standing in front of a Wooden Door.

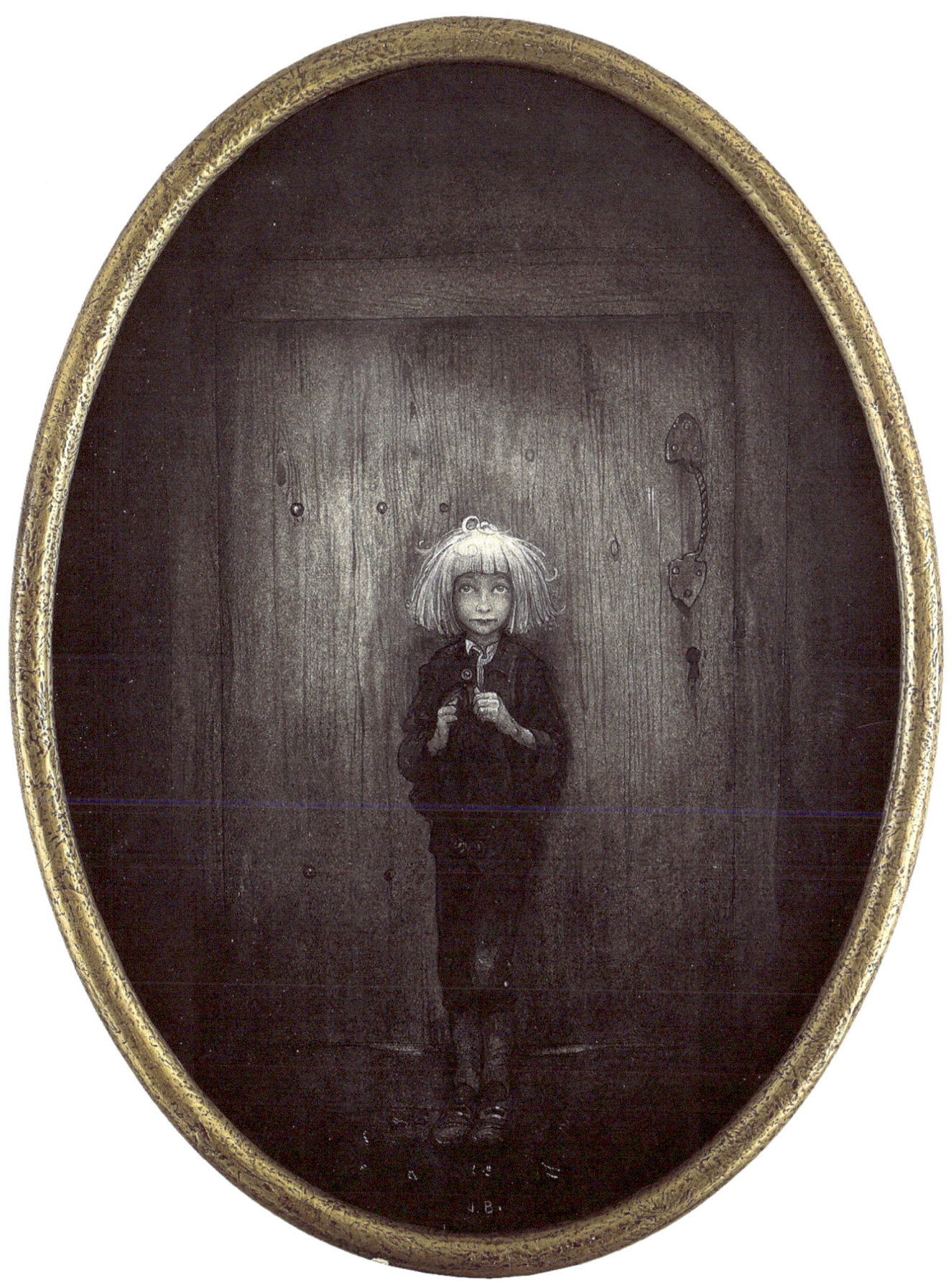

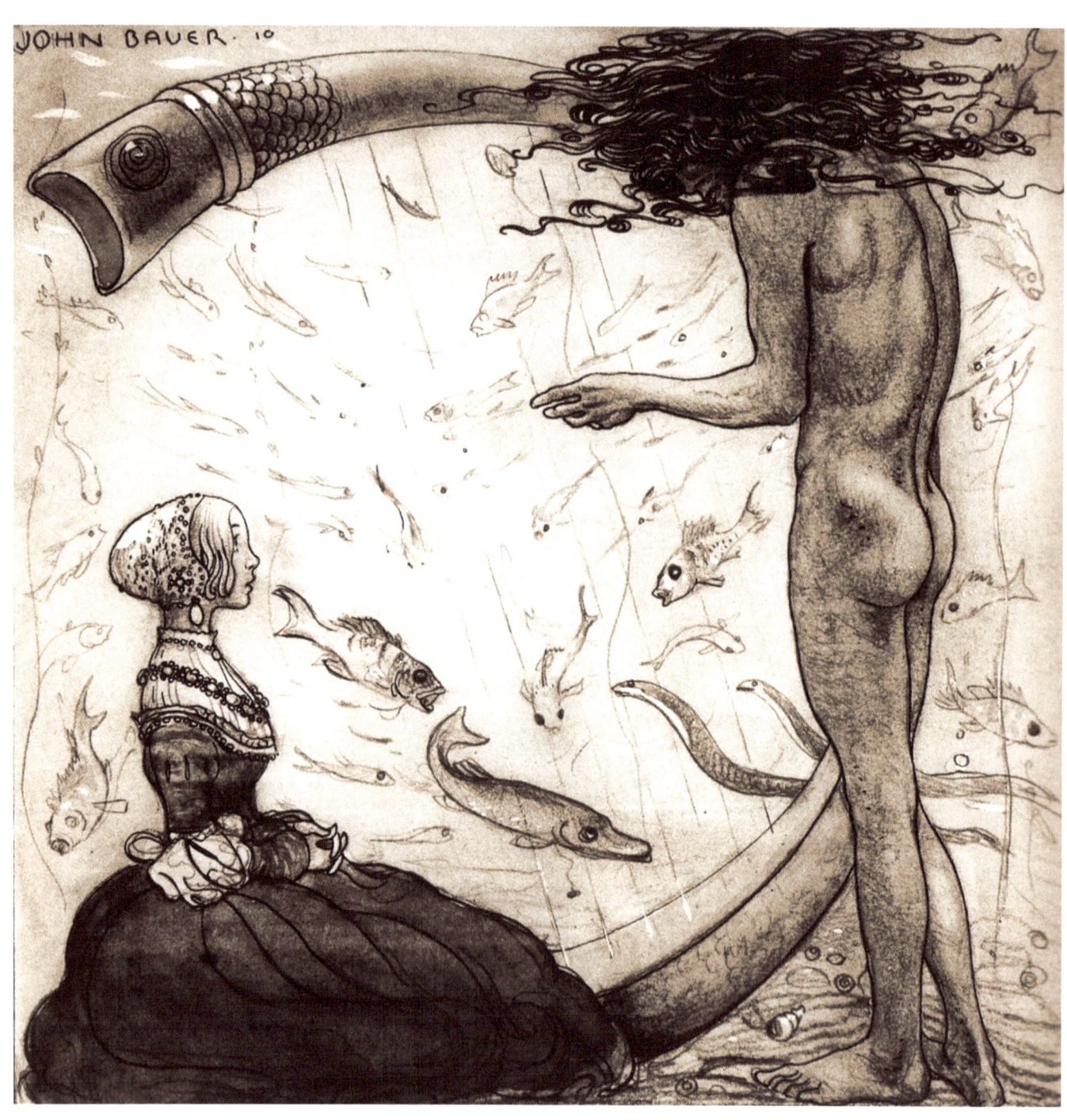

At first tone it was like something burst into Agna's heart.
From 'Agneta and The Sea King'

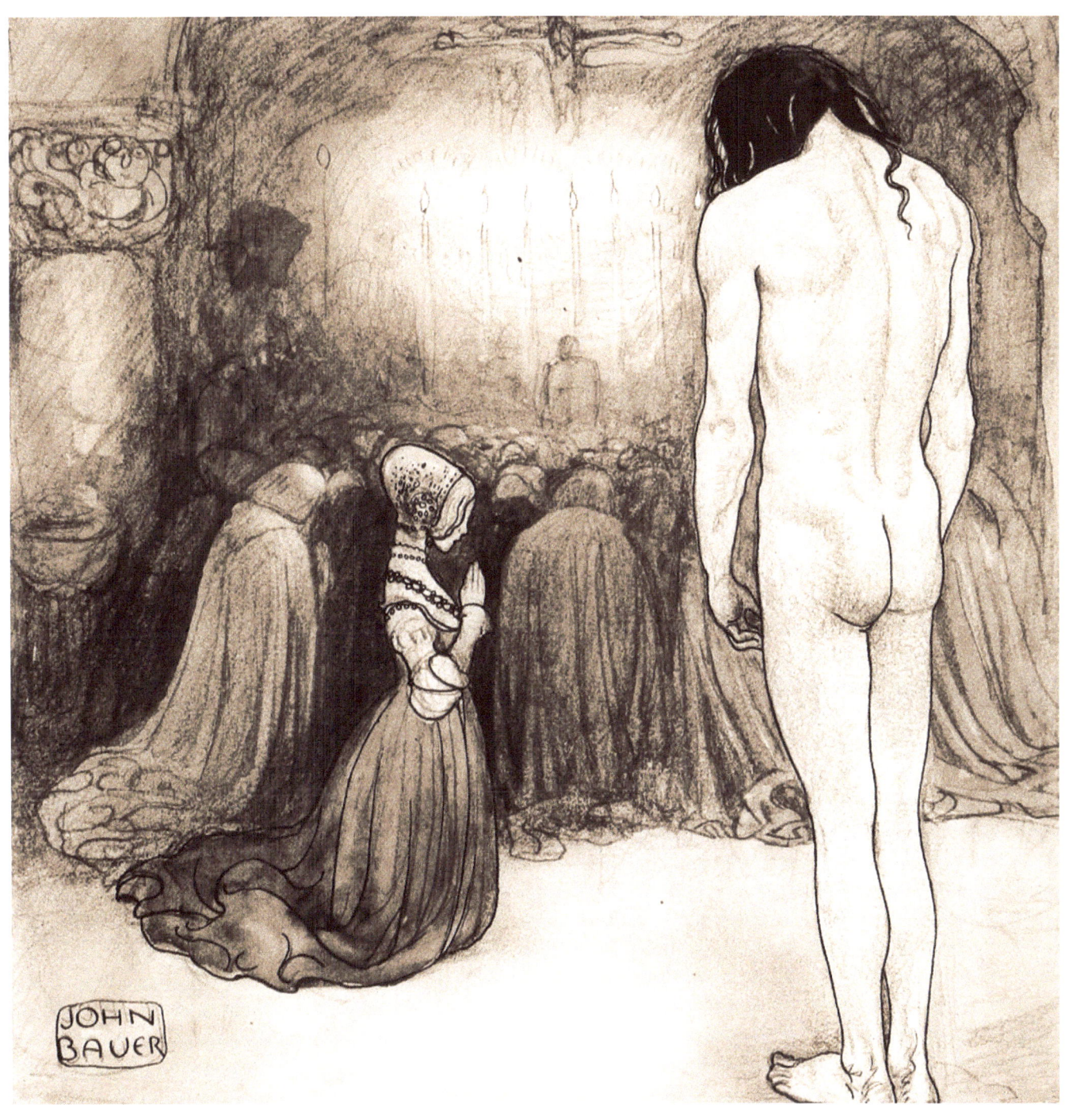

Now she noticed that the church door had opened, and there stood the Sea King.
From 'Agneta and The Sea King'

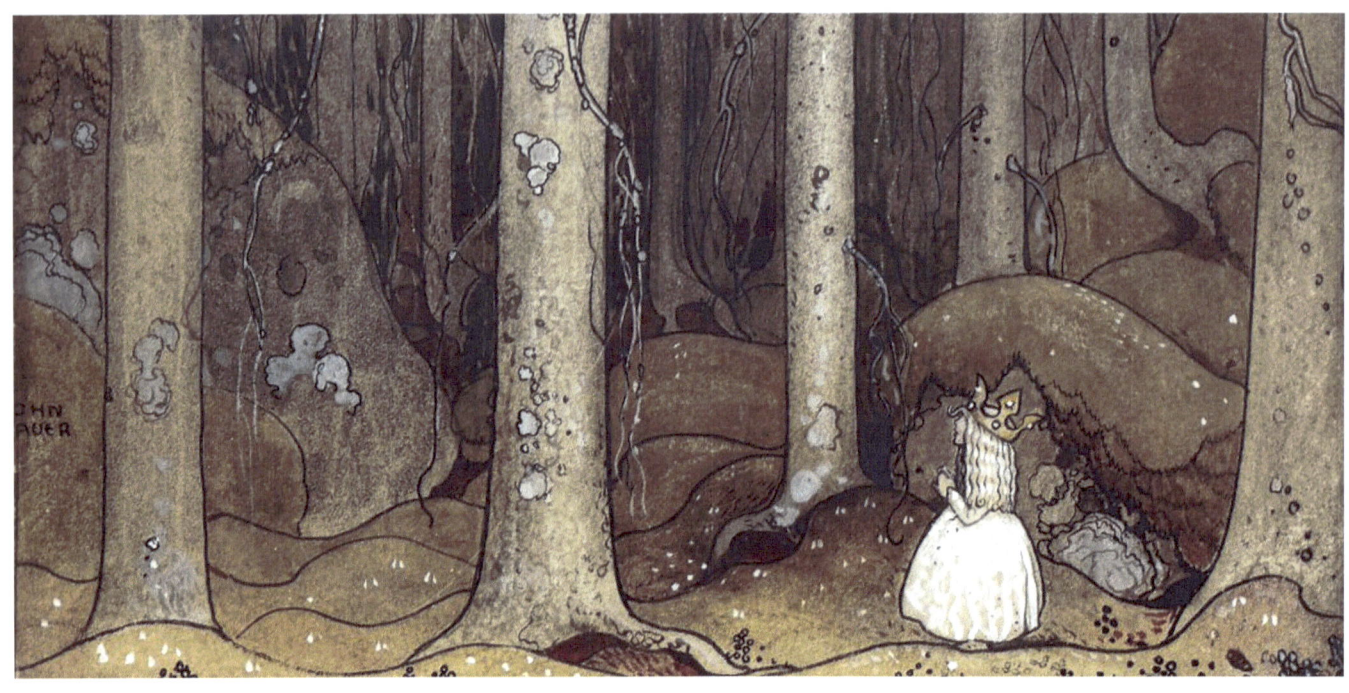

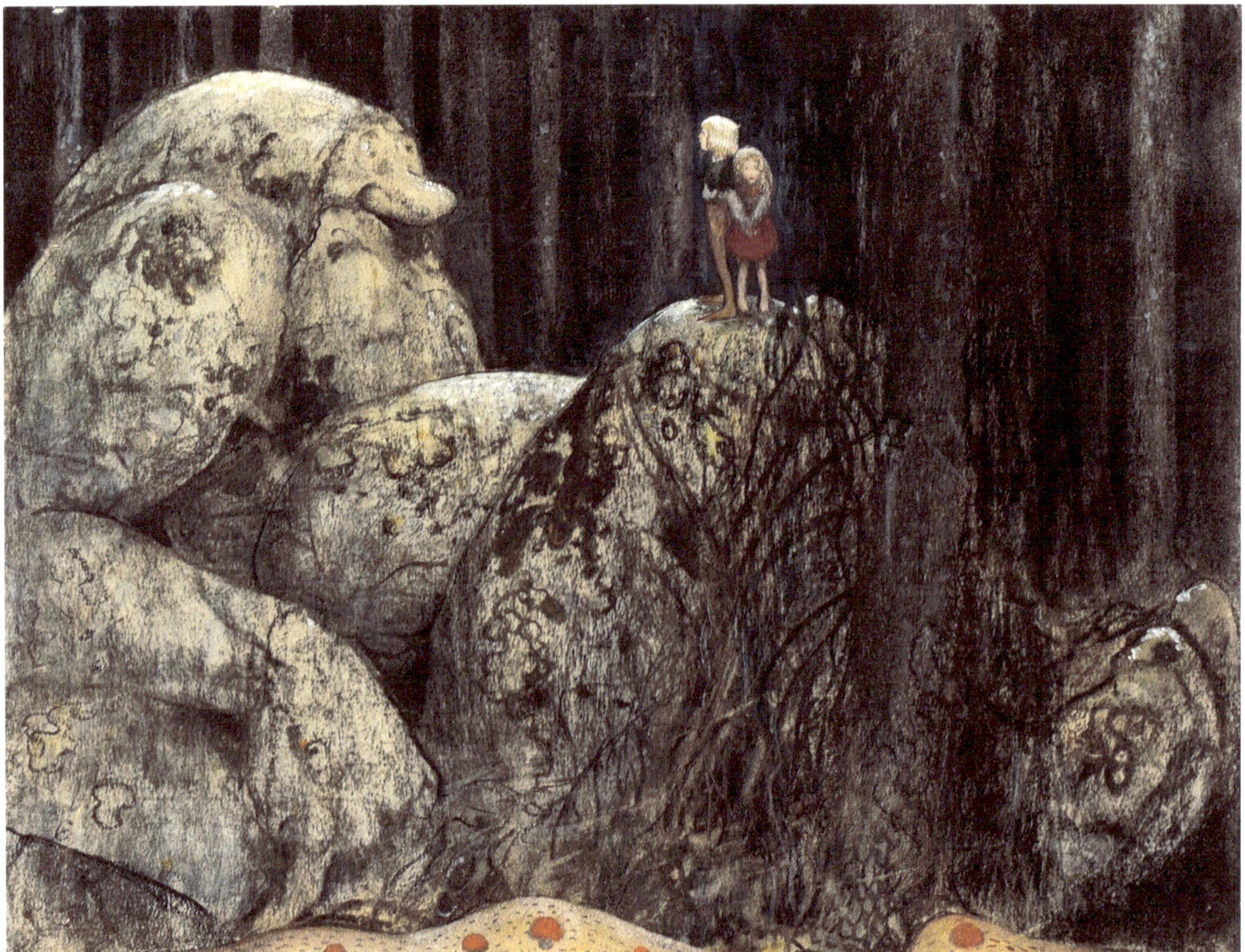

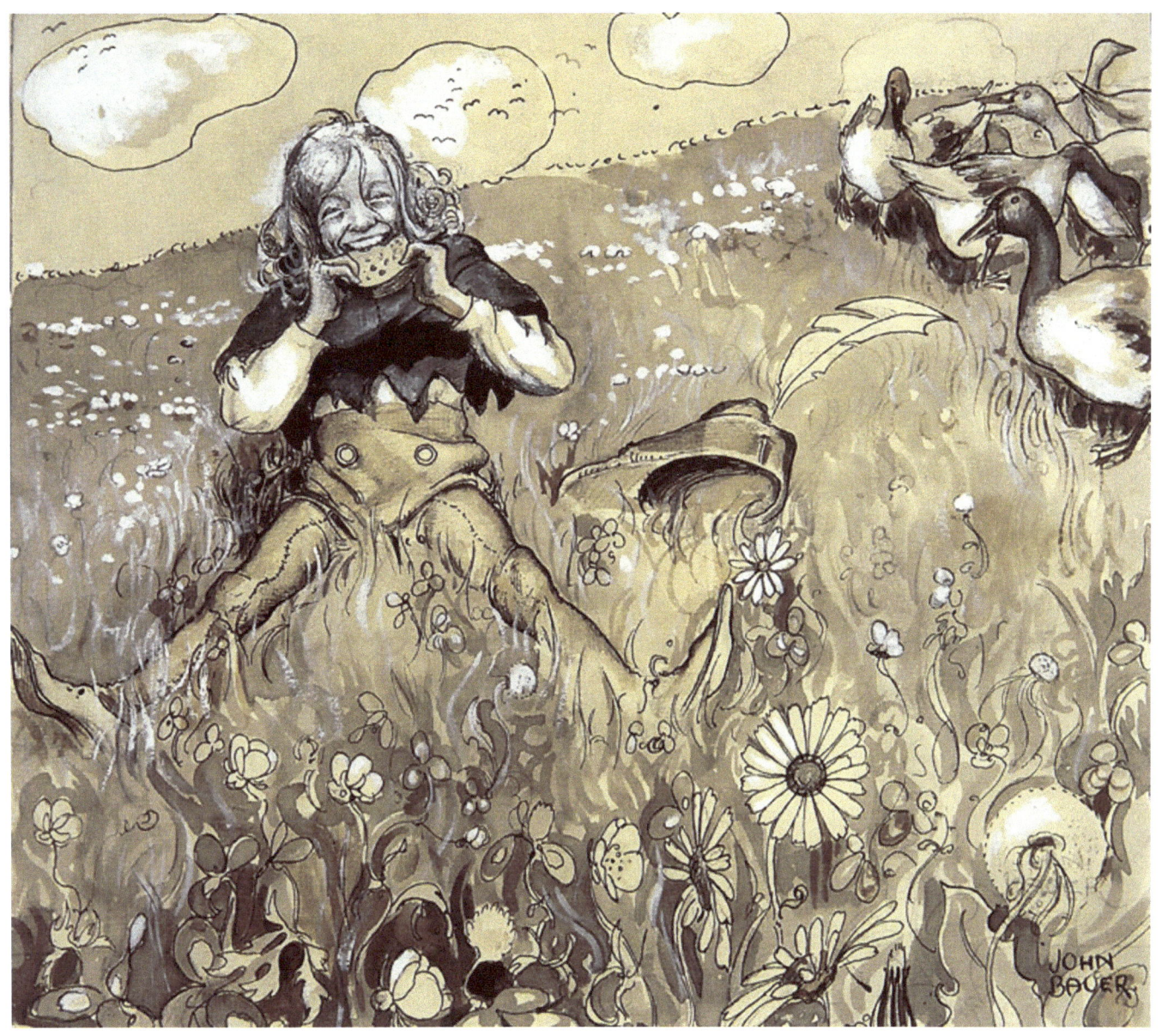

Above: The Four Aunts.

Top Right: "It's beautiful here," she said, clapping her hands together.

Bottom left: The Child and the Stone Troll.

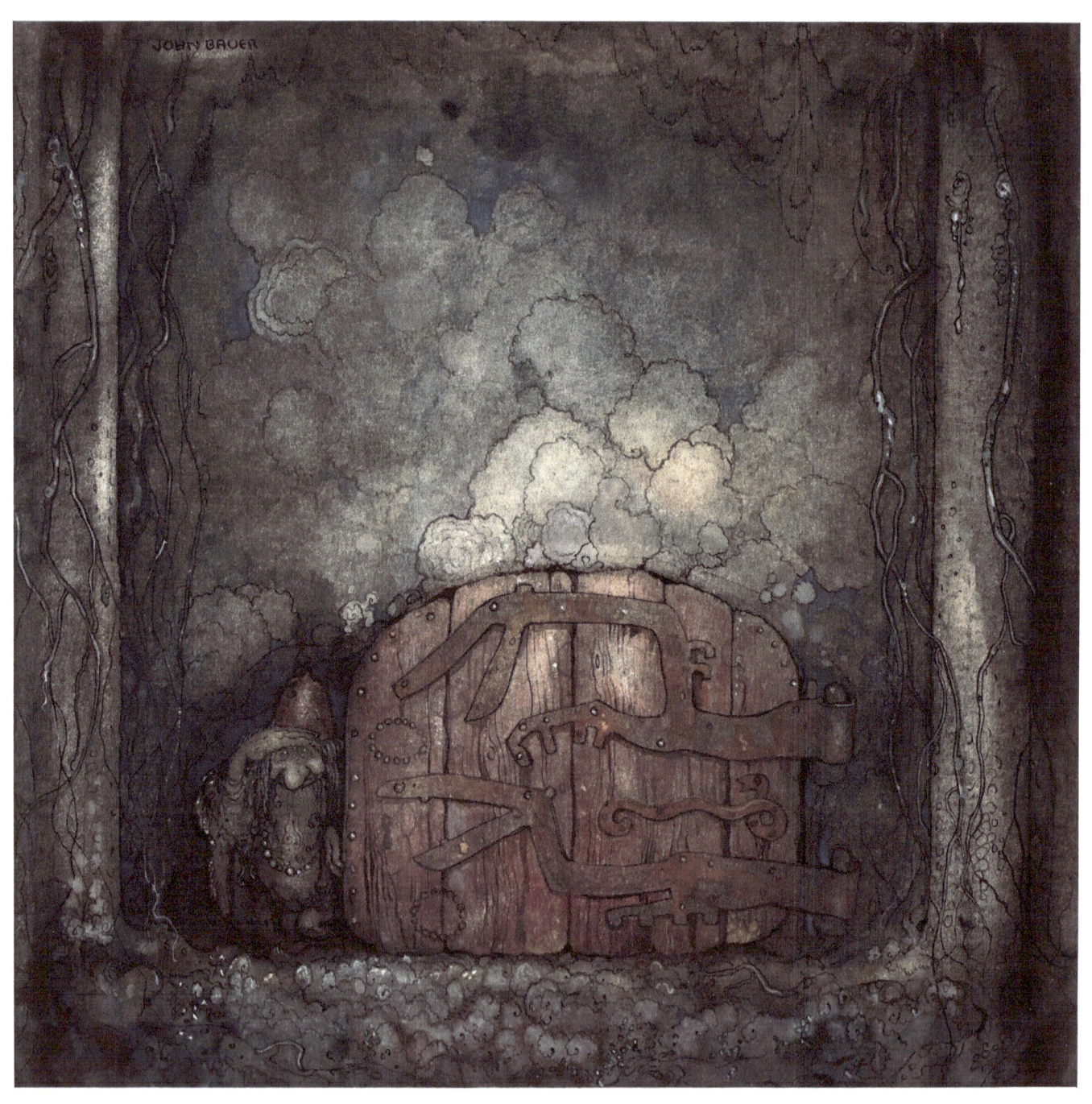

Mountain Gates

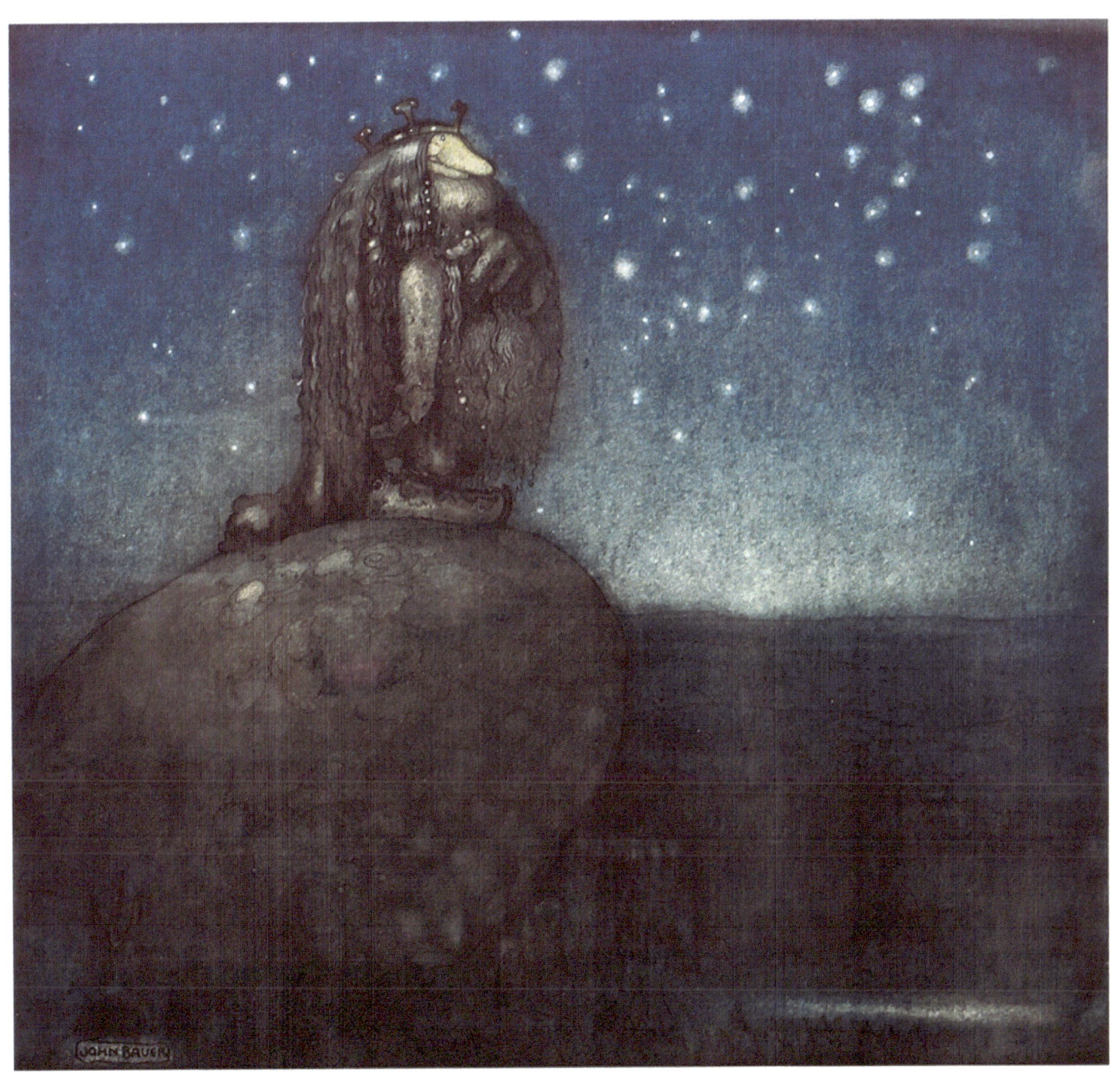

A Mountain Troll

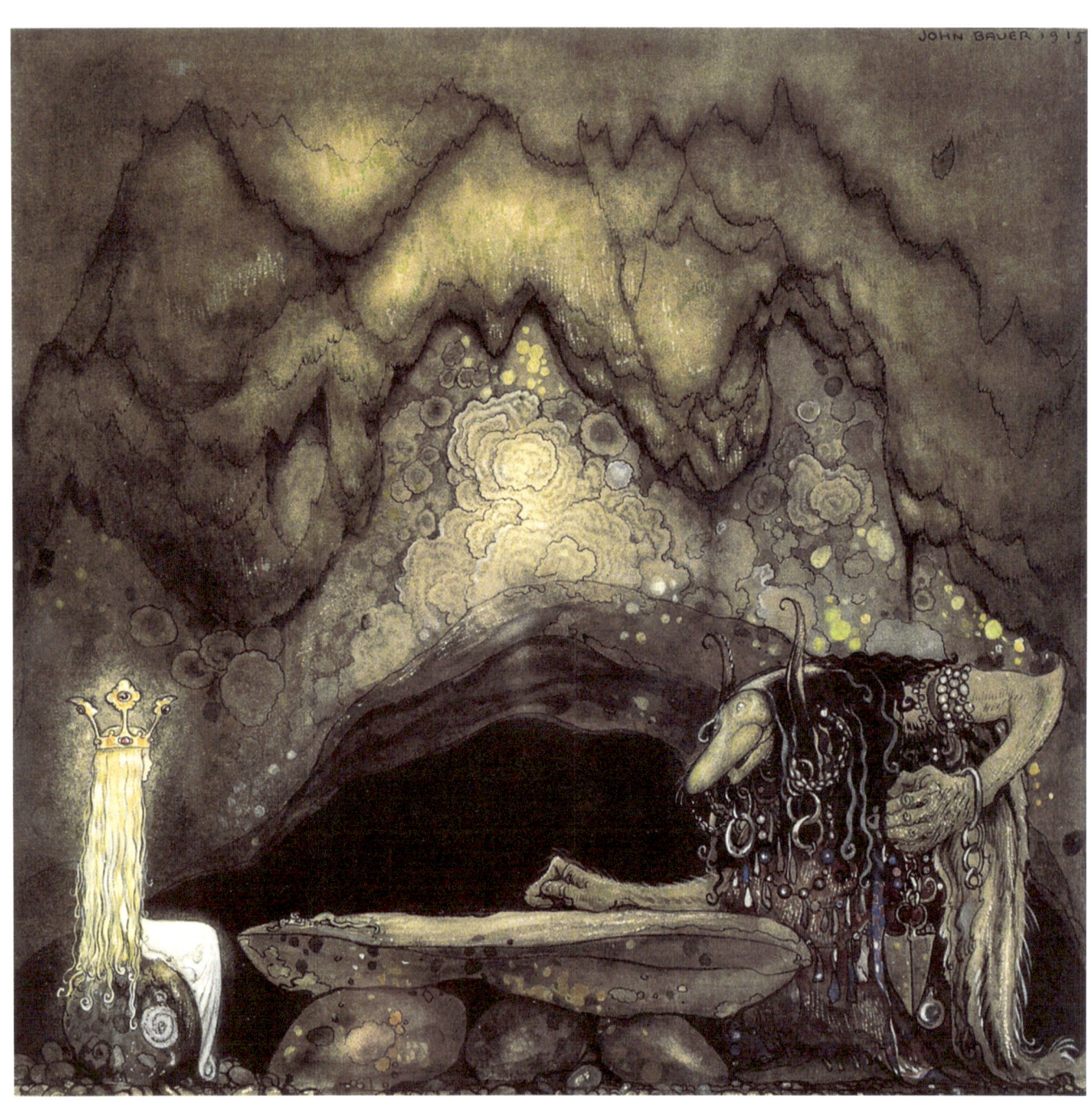

Well, how about the appetite? continued the sorcerer.
From 'The Troll Mother Seeks a Wife'

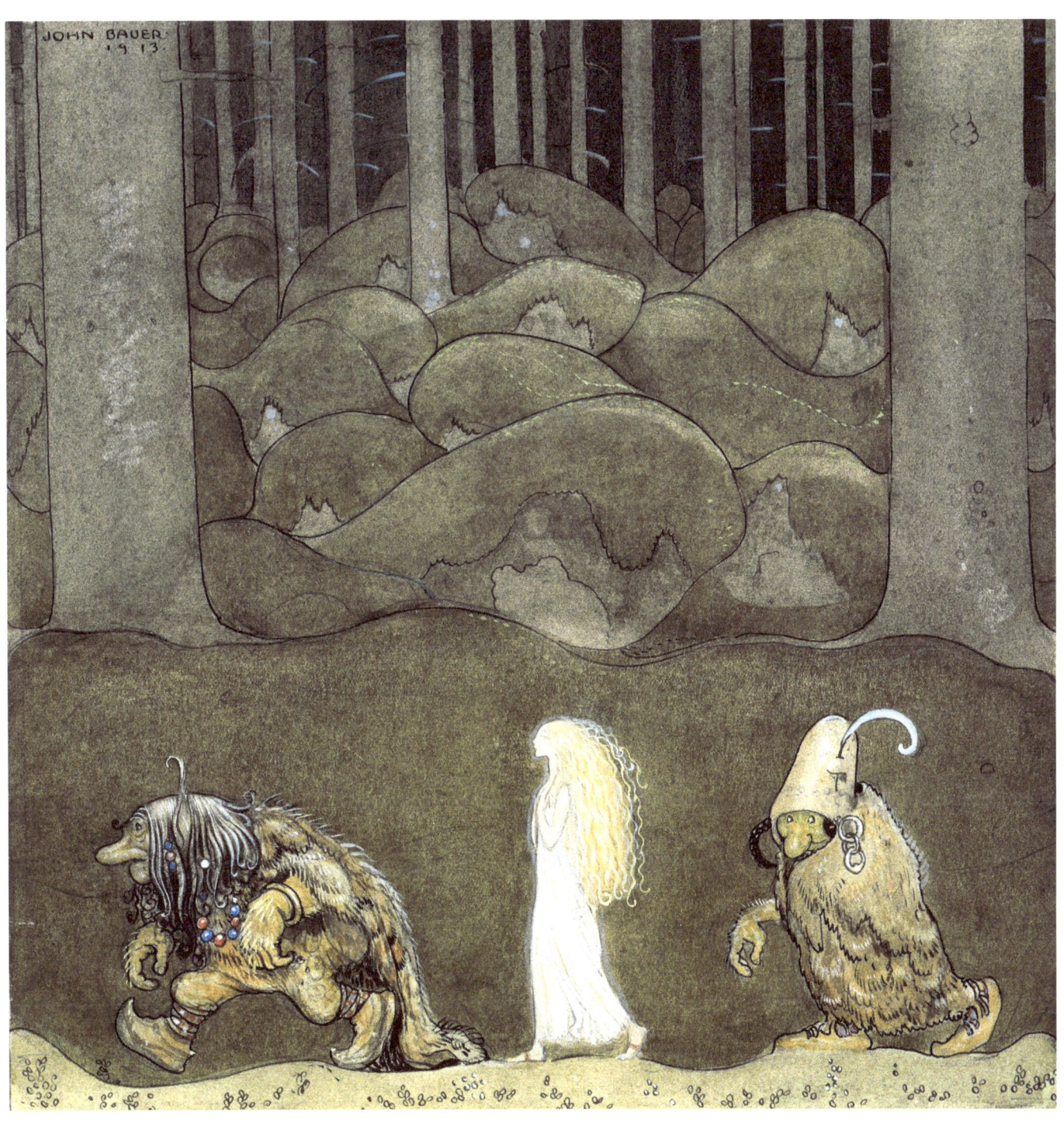

One evening around midsummer, they went with Bianca Maria deep into the forest.
From 'The Changlings'

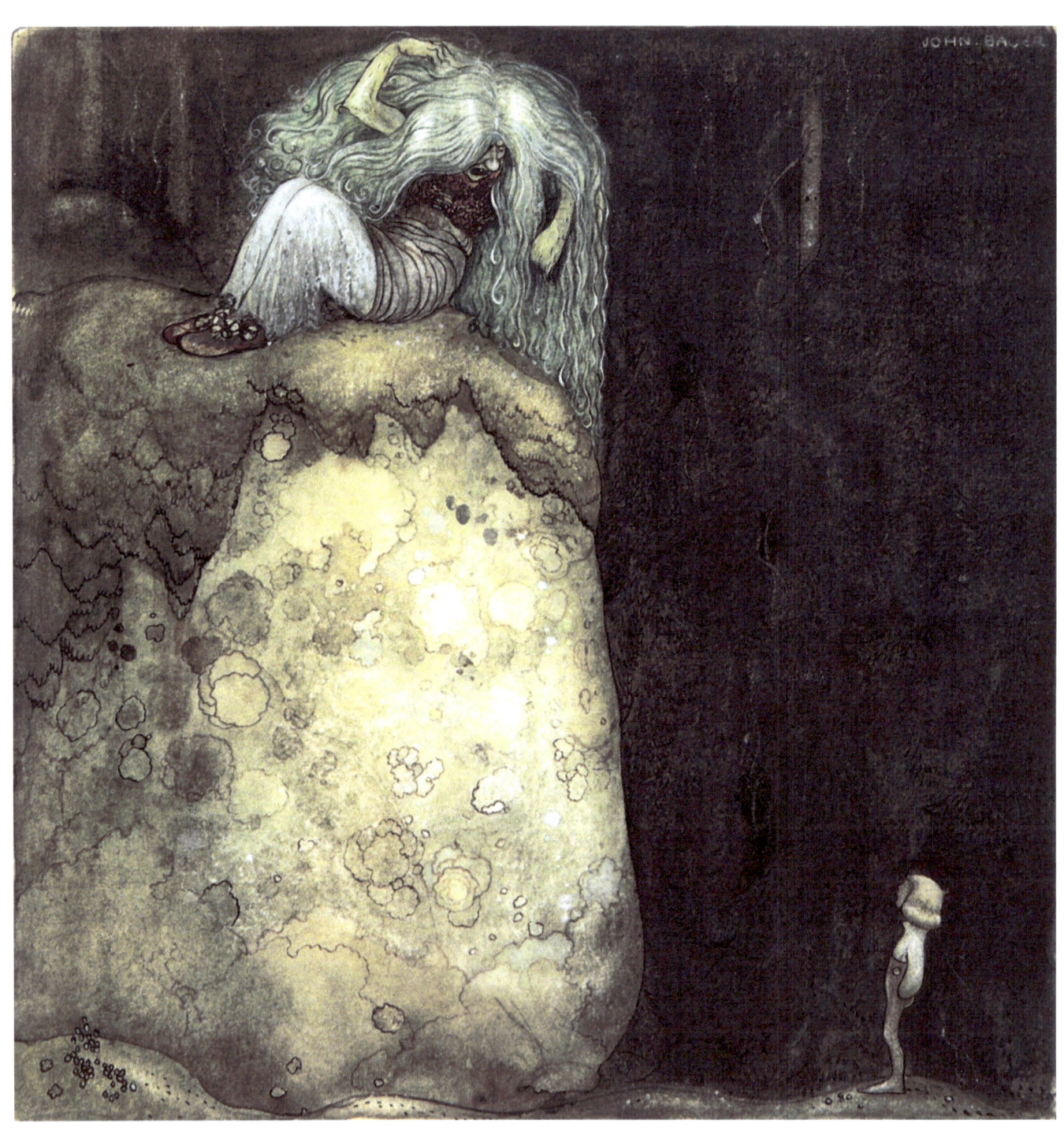

From 'The Boy Who Was Never Afraid'

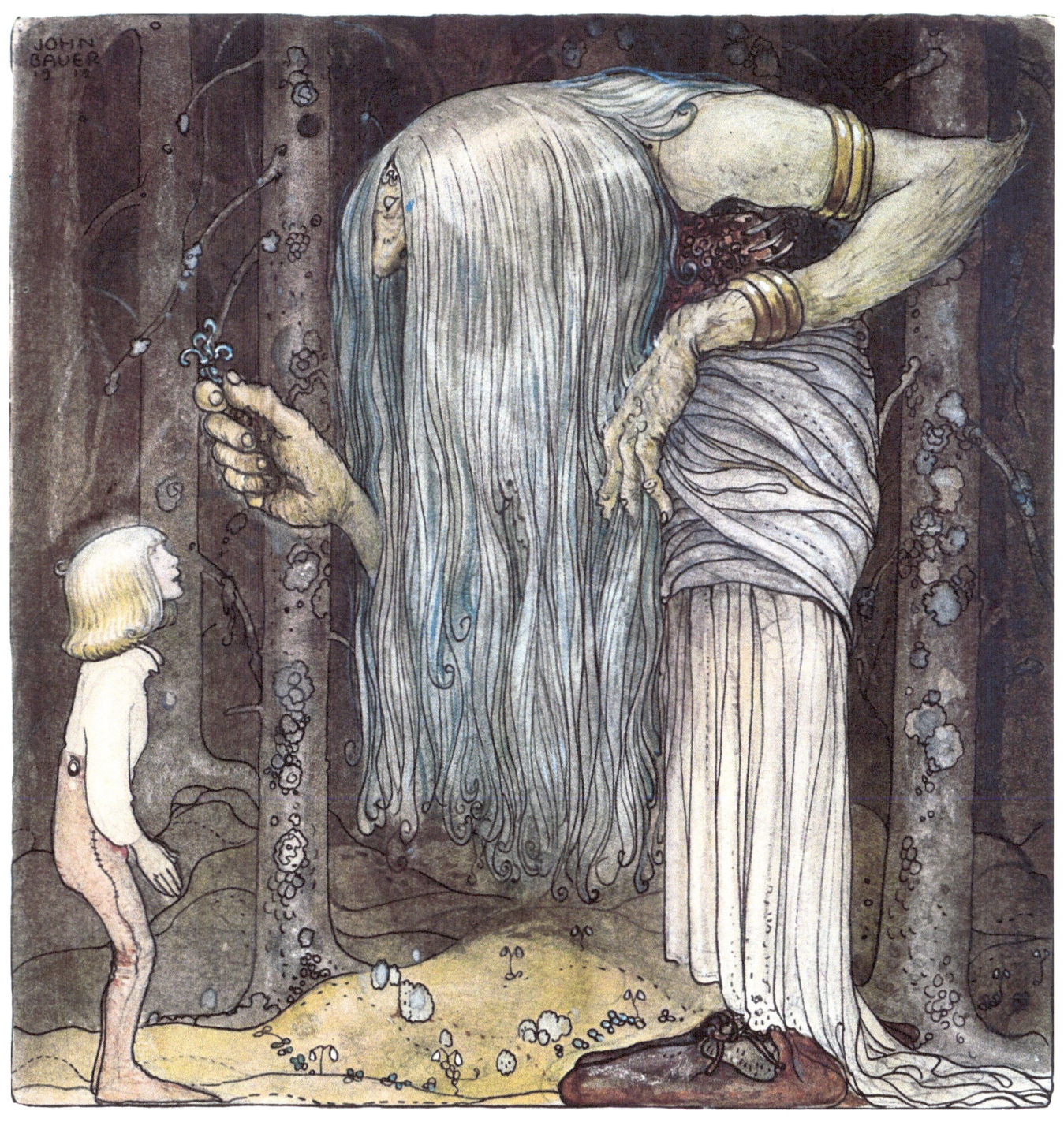

"Here is a piece of a troll herb which nobody else but me can find."
From 'The Boy Who Was Never Afraid'

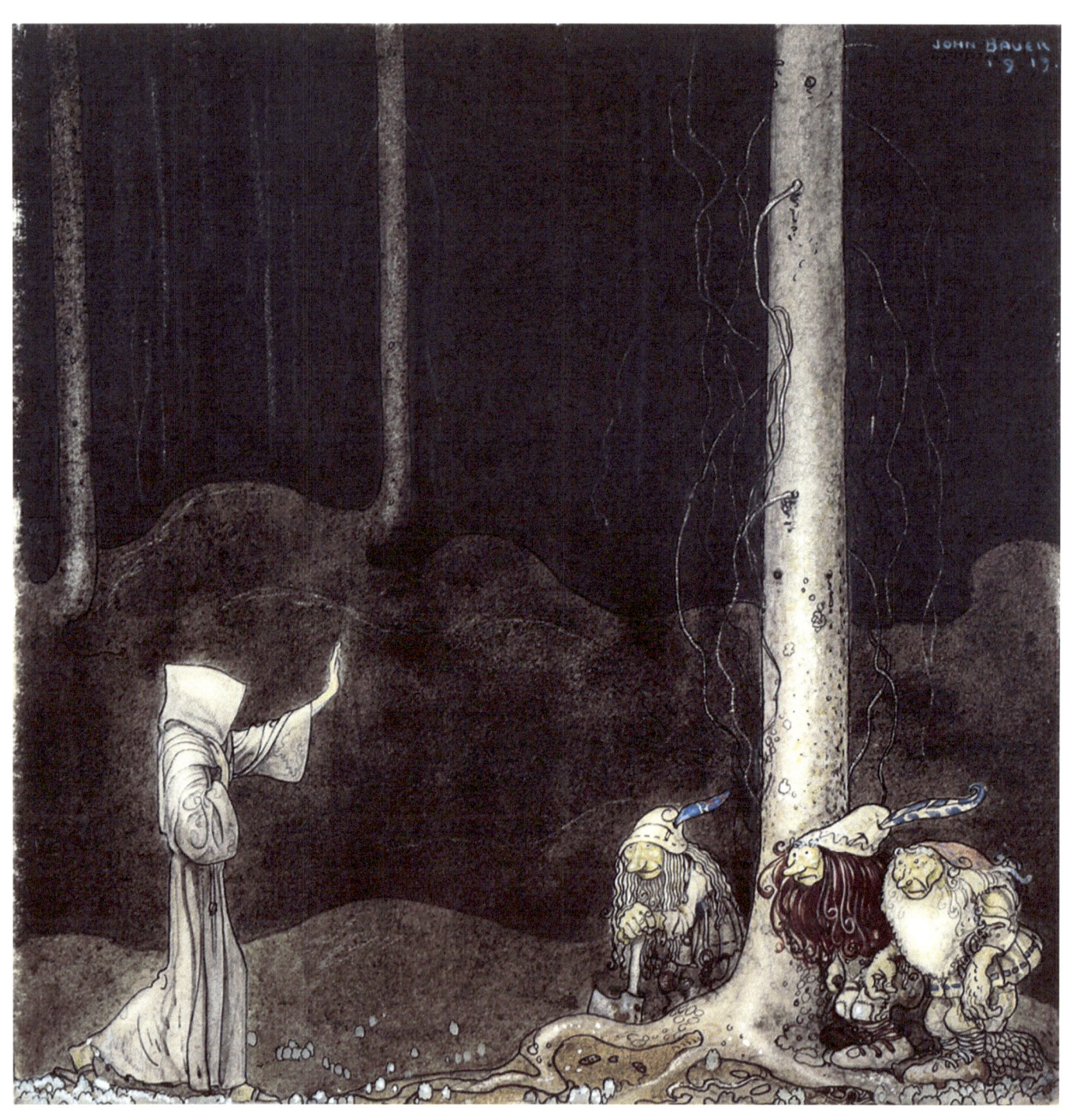

From 'Brother Martin'

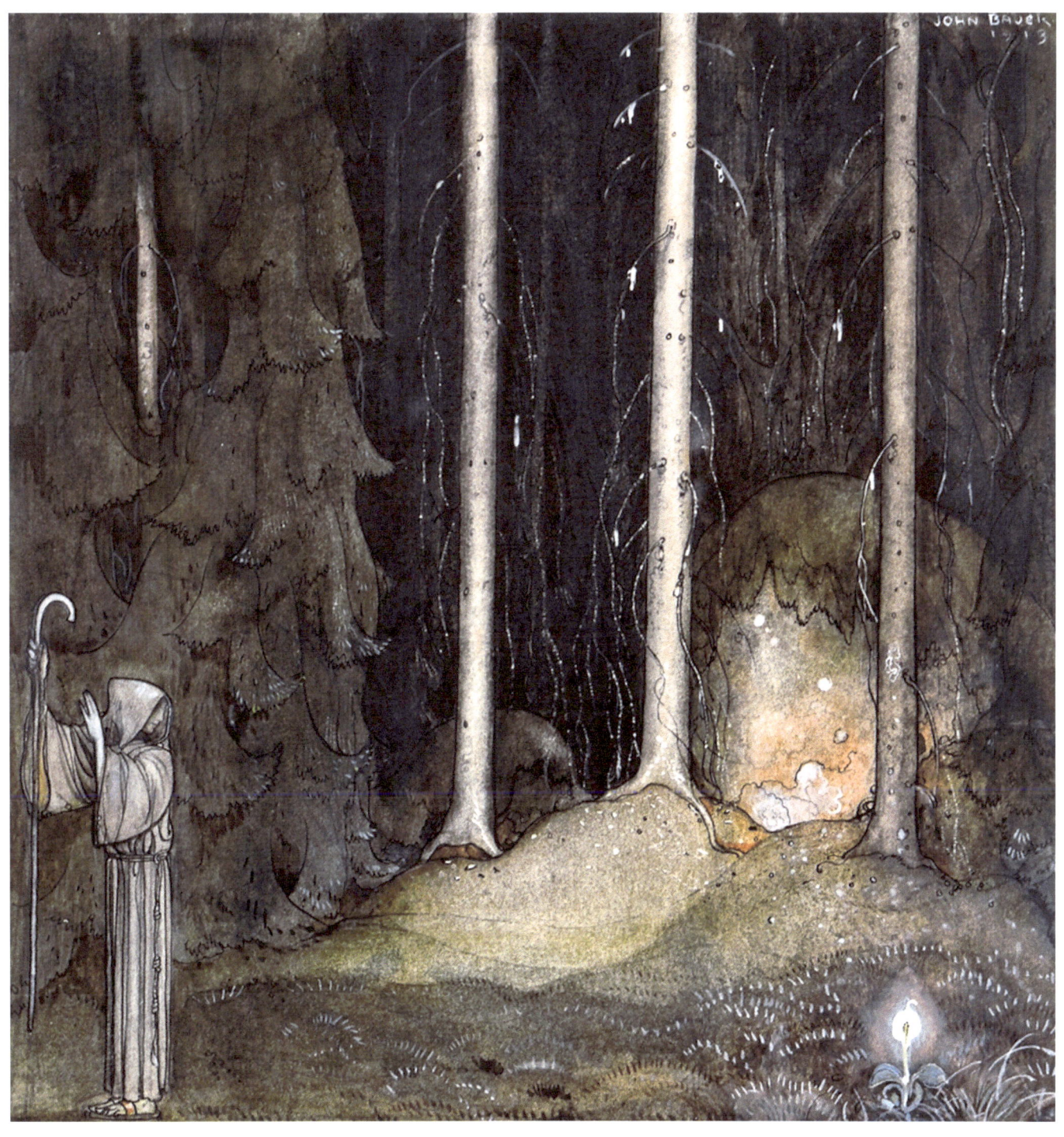

From 'Brother Martin'

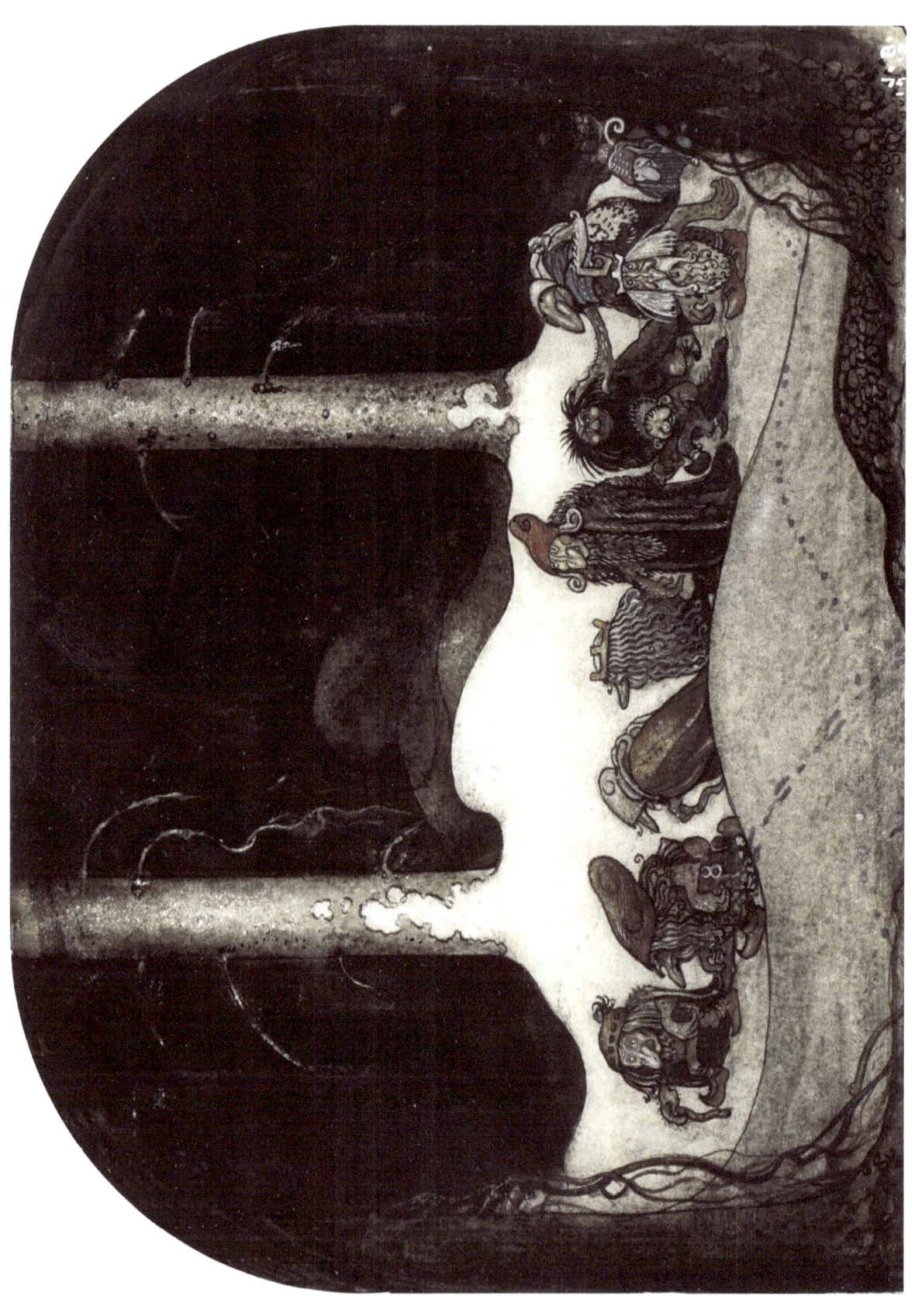

In the Christmas Night

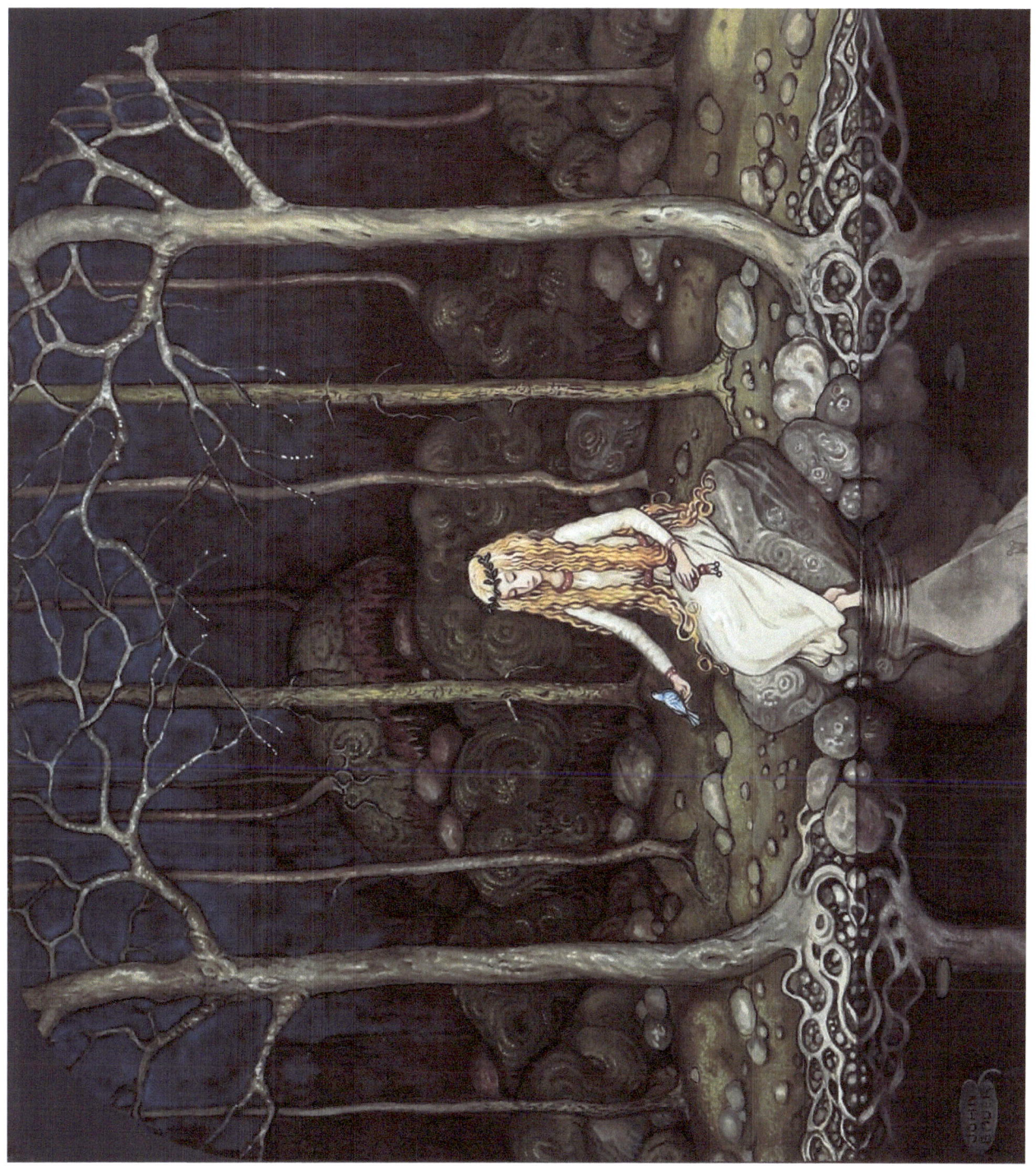

The Tale of the Moose Hop and the Little Princess Cotton Grass

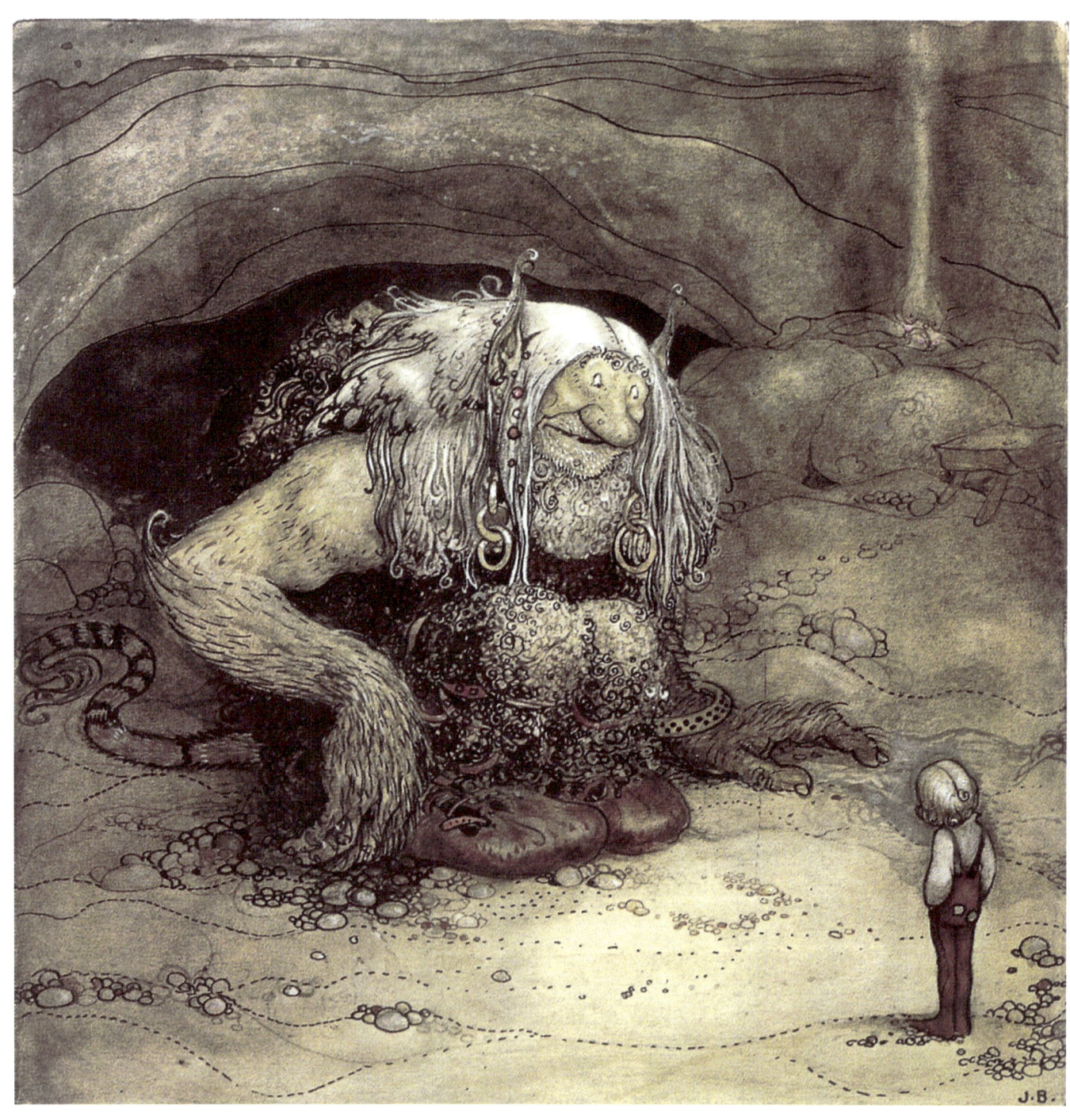

Above: "Oh my, What a little runt!" exclaimed the Troll.
From 'The Boy Who Was Never Afraid'

Right: The Giant Who Slept for Ten Thousand Years

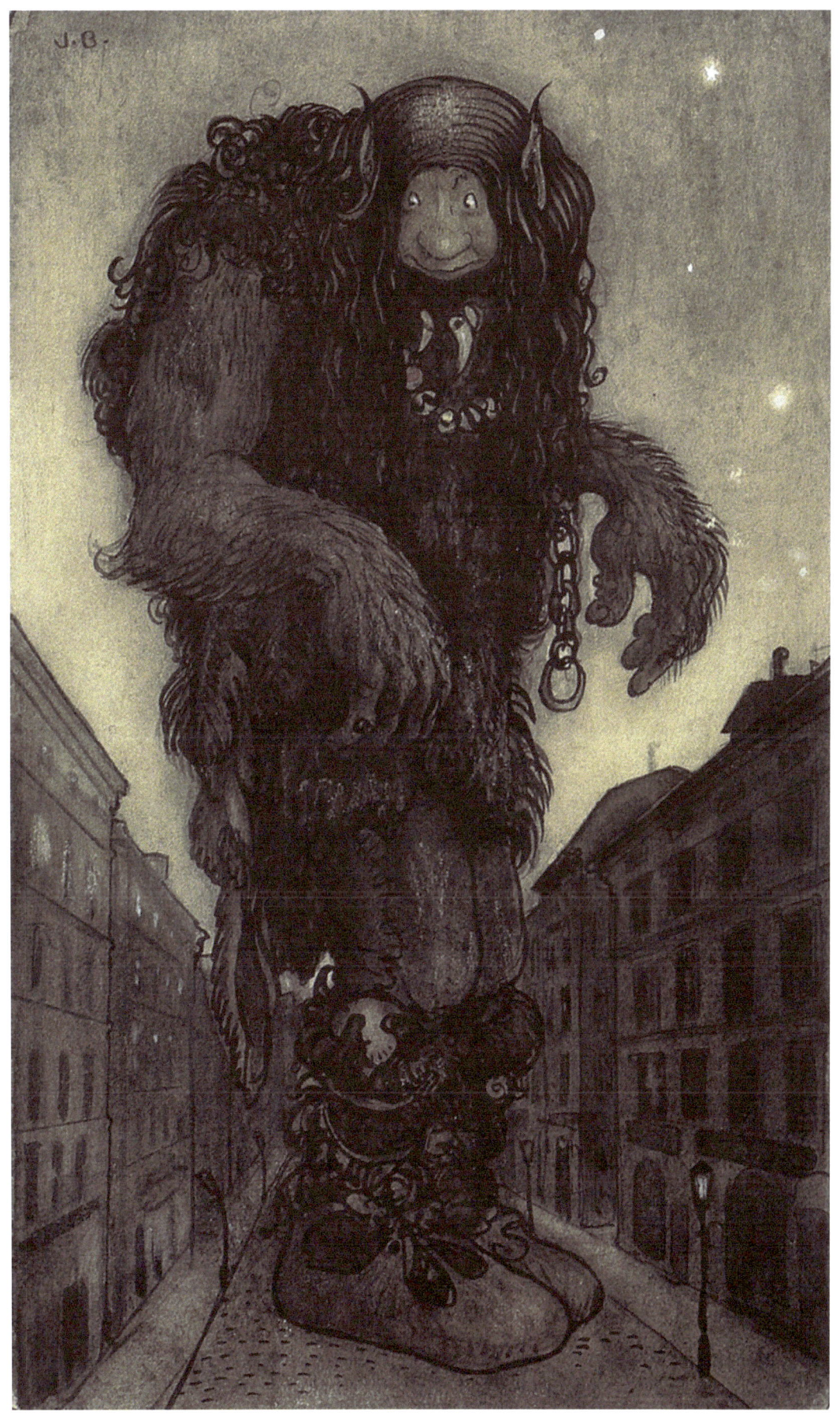

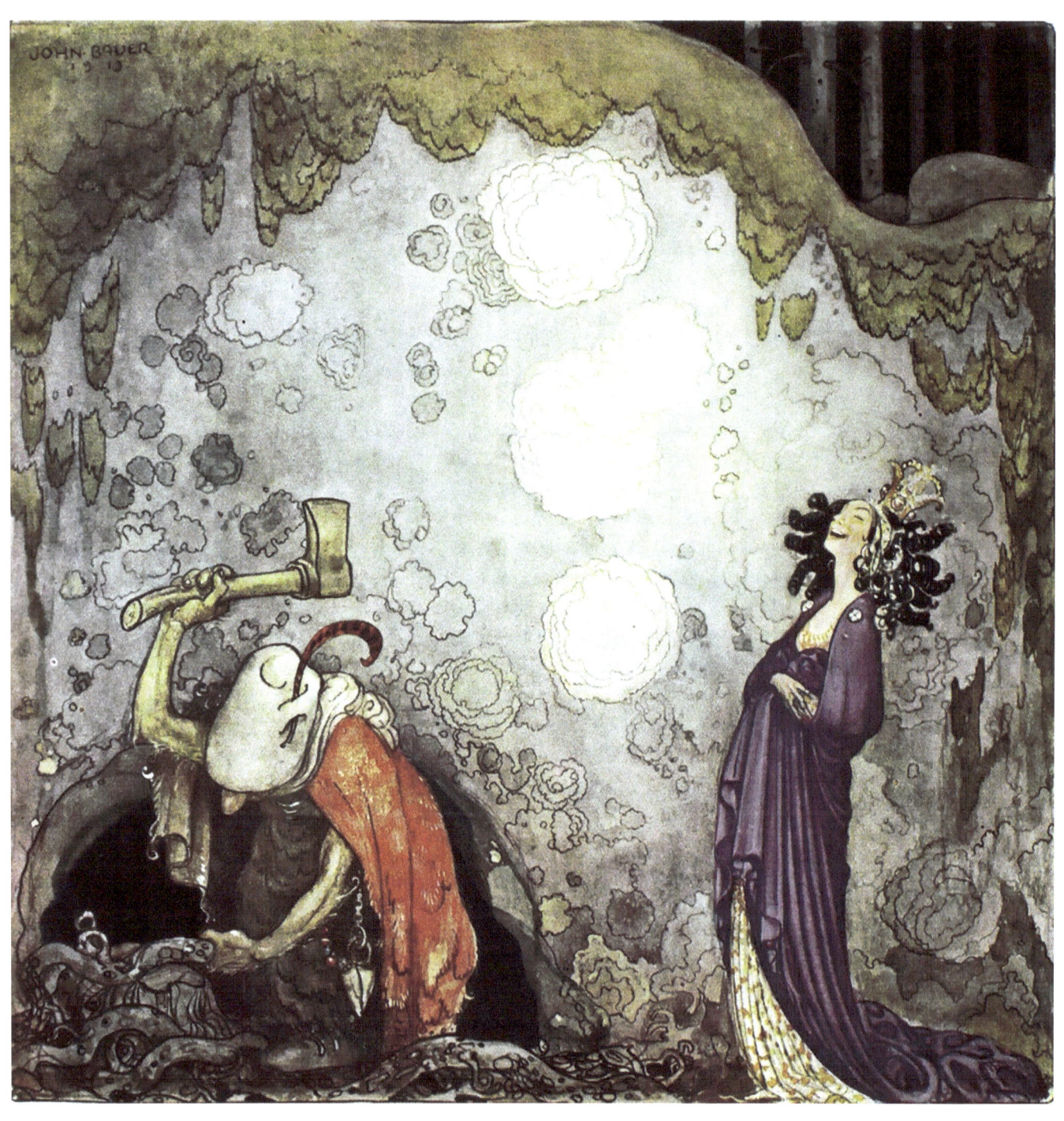
From 'The Changelings'

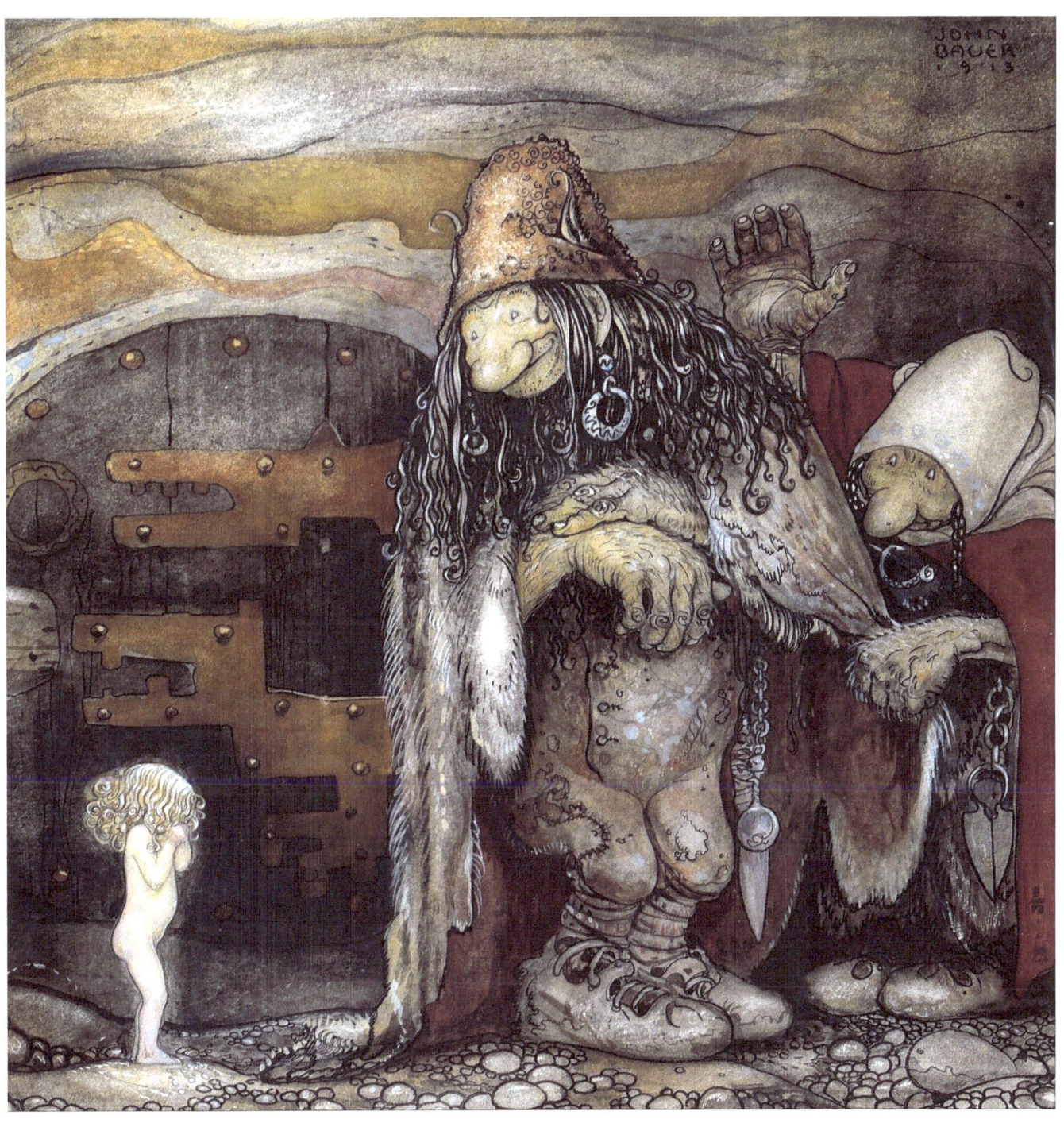

From 'The Changelings'

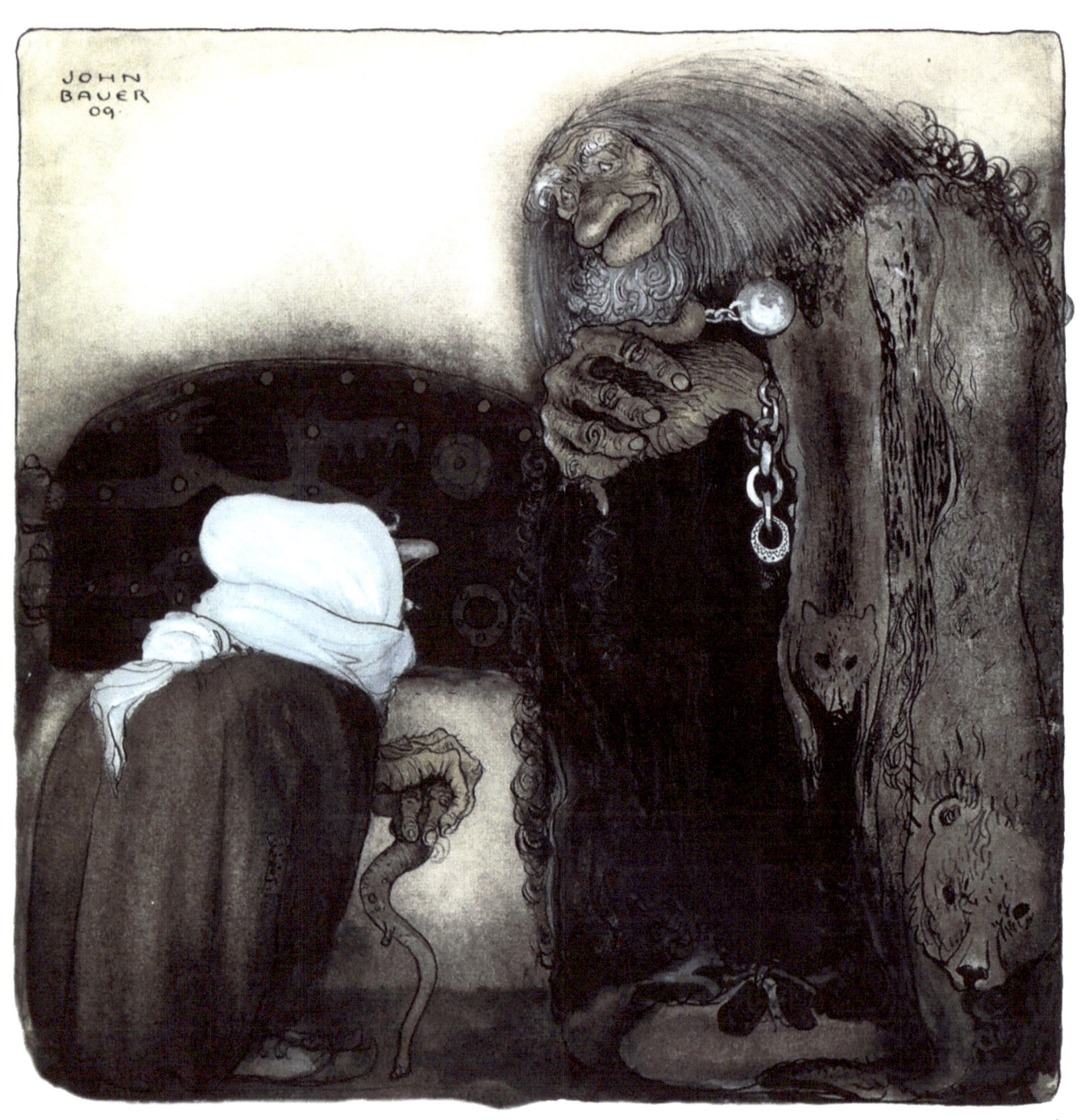

From 'The Four Big Trolls and Little Peter Pastureman'

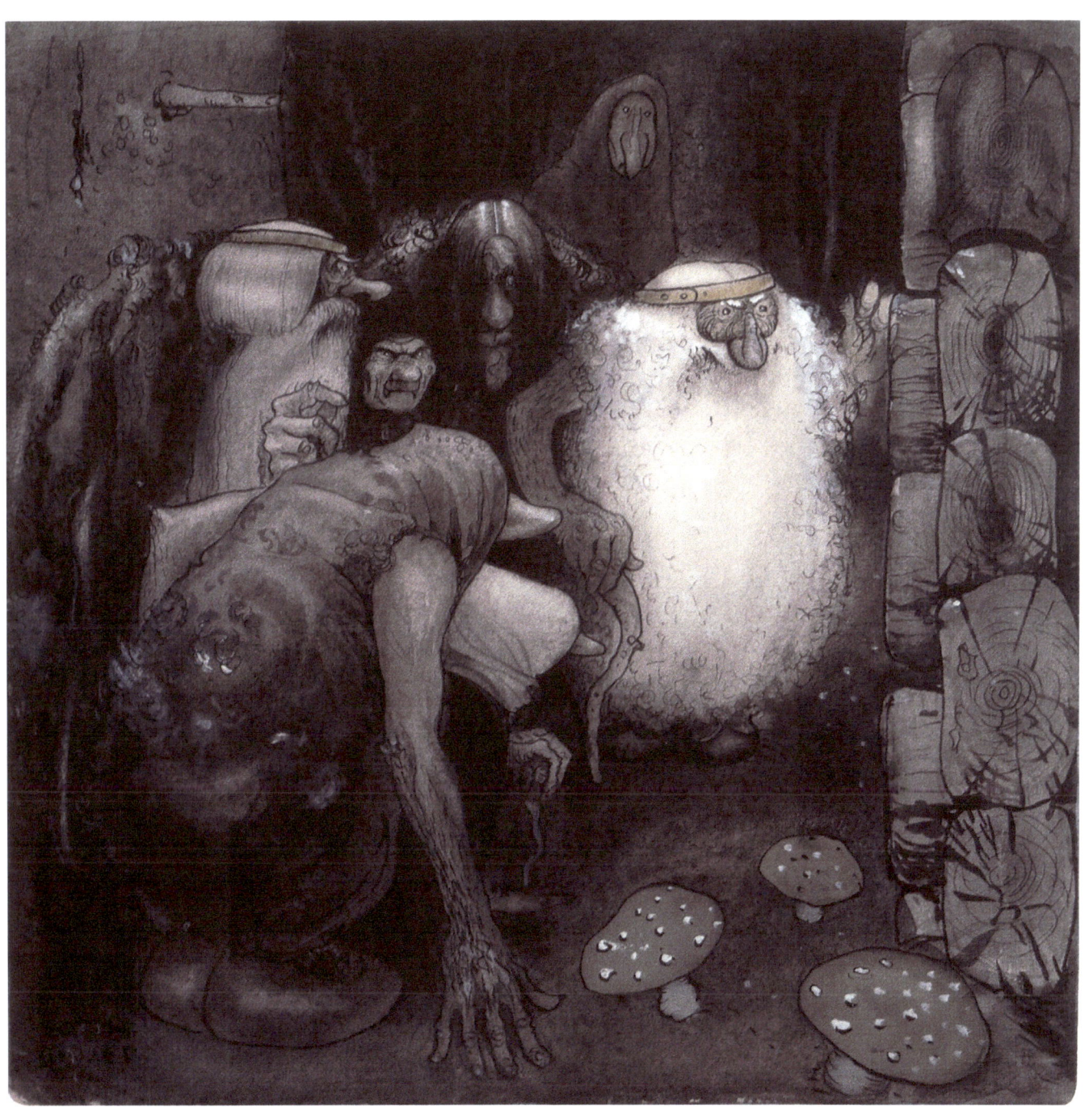

From 'The Four Big Trolls and Little Peter Pastureman'

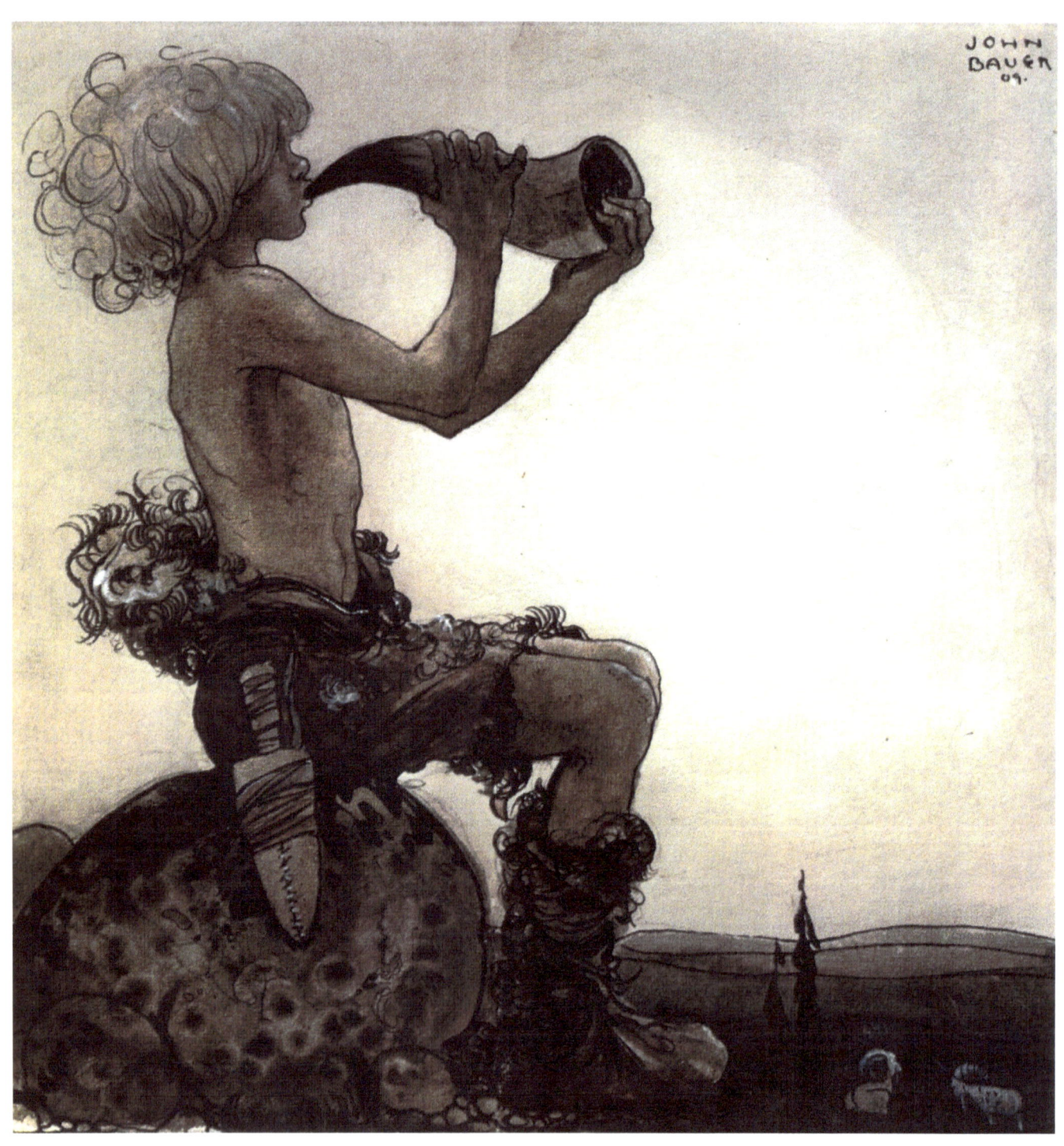

From 'The Four Big Trolls and Little Peter Pastureman'

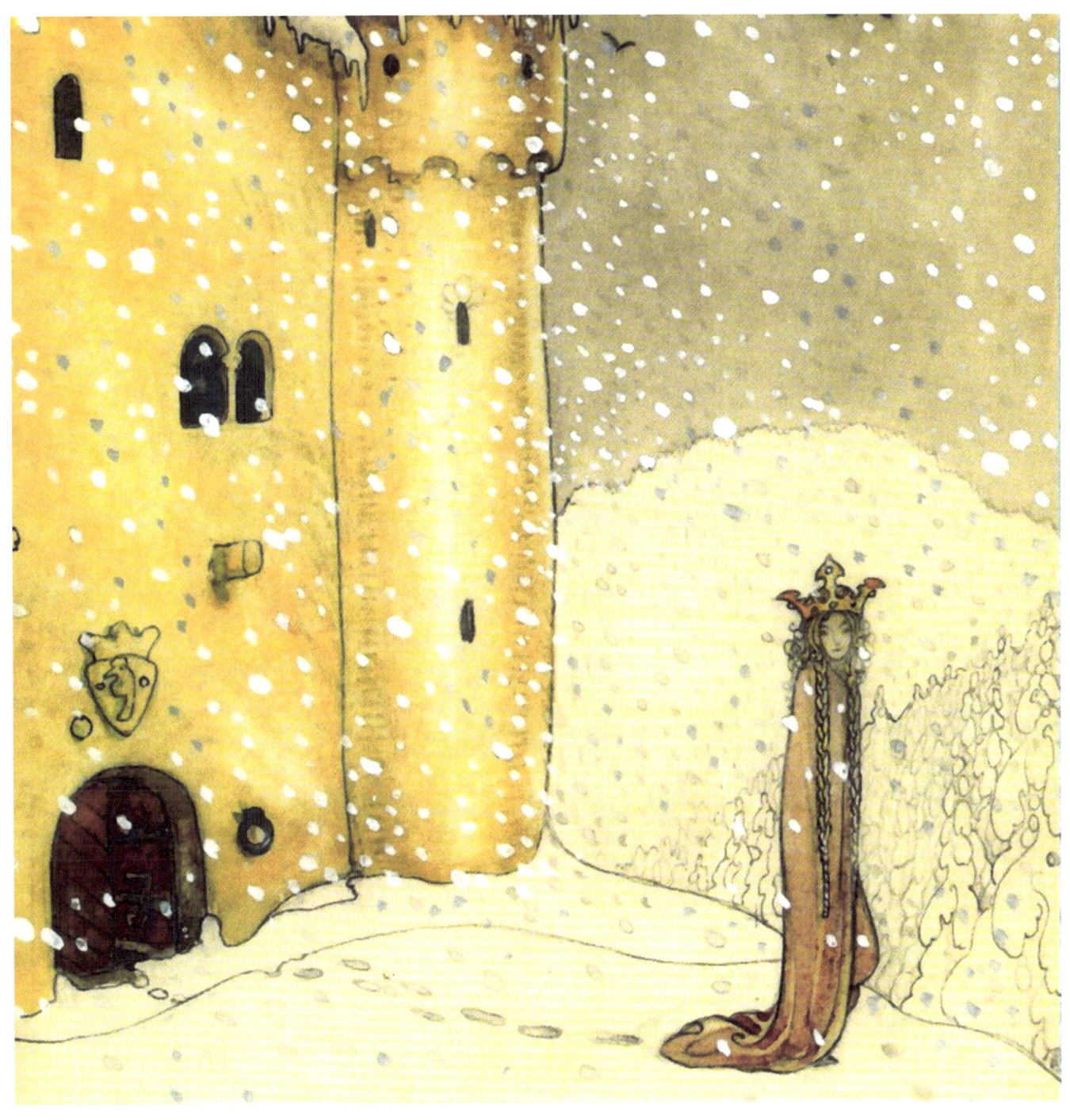

The Golden Castle

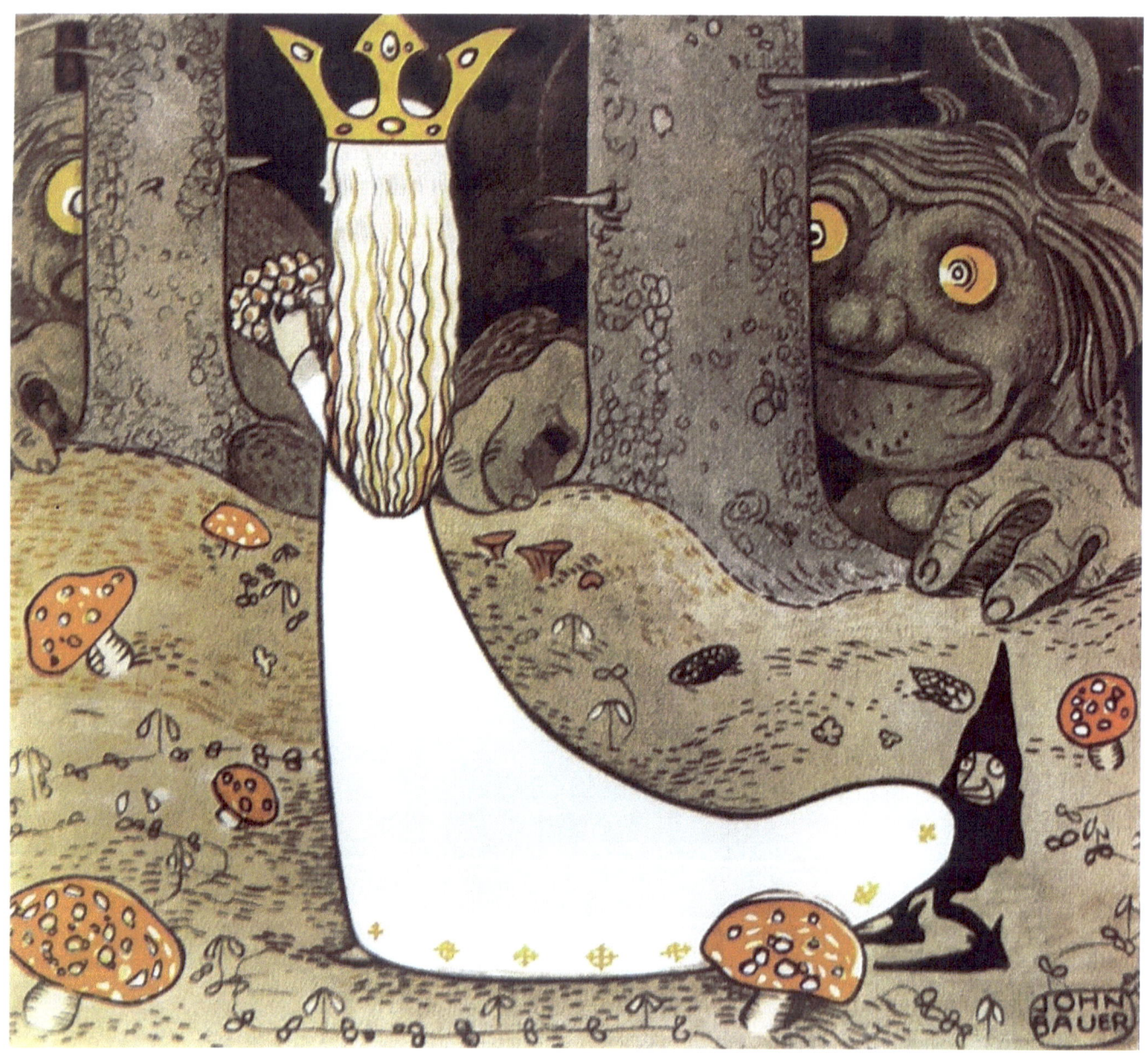

Above: Princess Daga watched by Trolls.

Right, Top left: Princess Tuvstarr in the Field. Top right: The Boy and the Raven.

Bottom right: The Trolls in Domberget expected visiting Strangers.

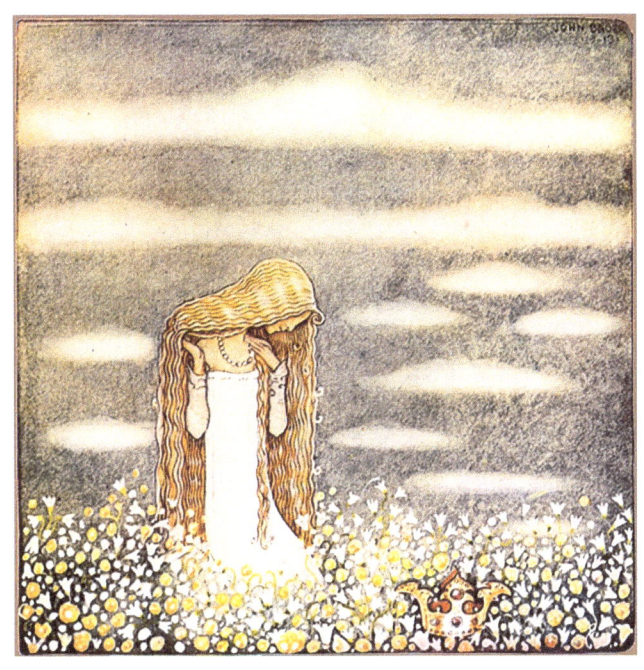
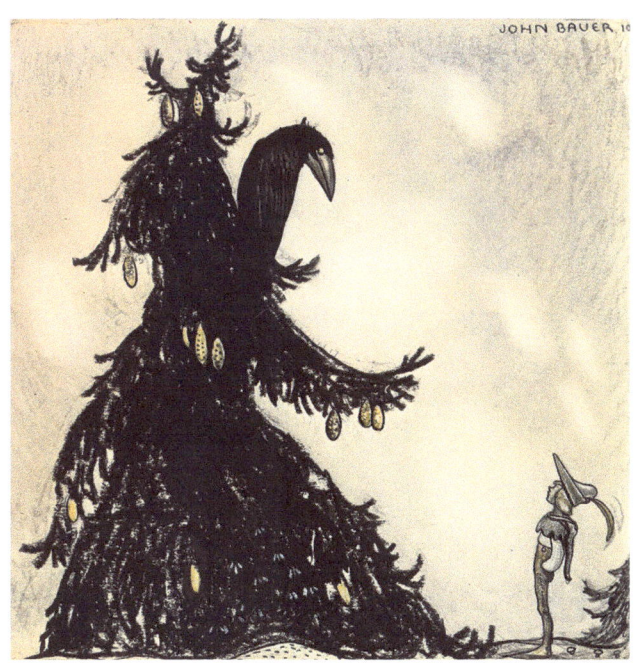

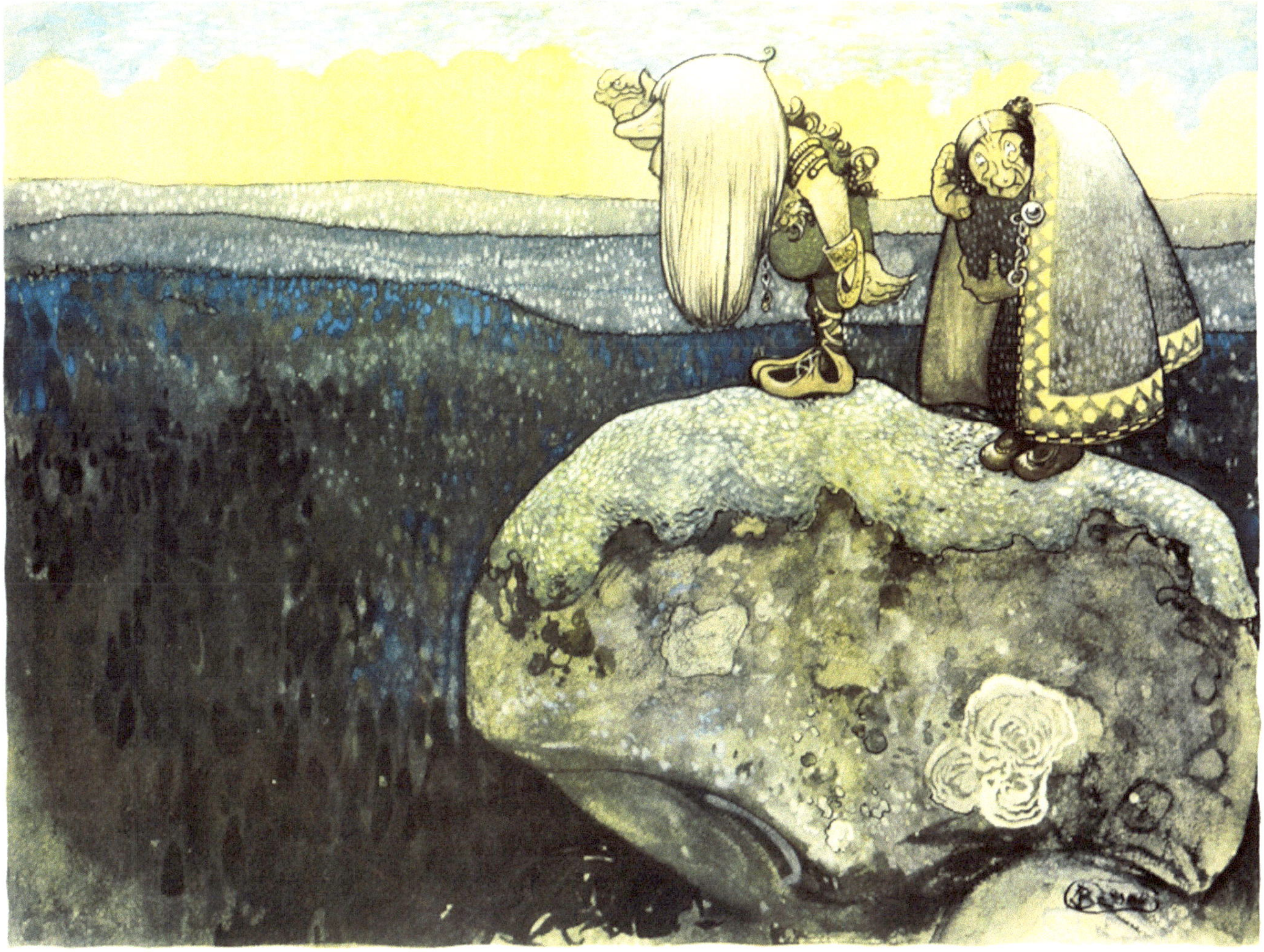

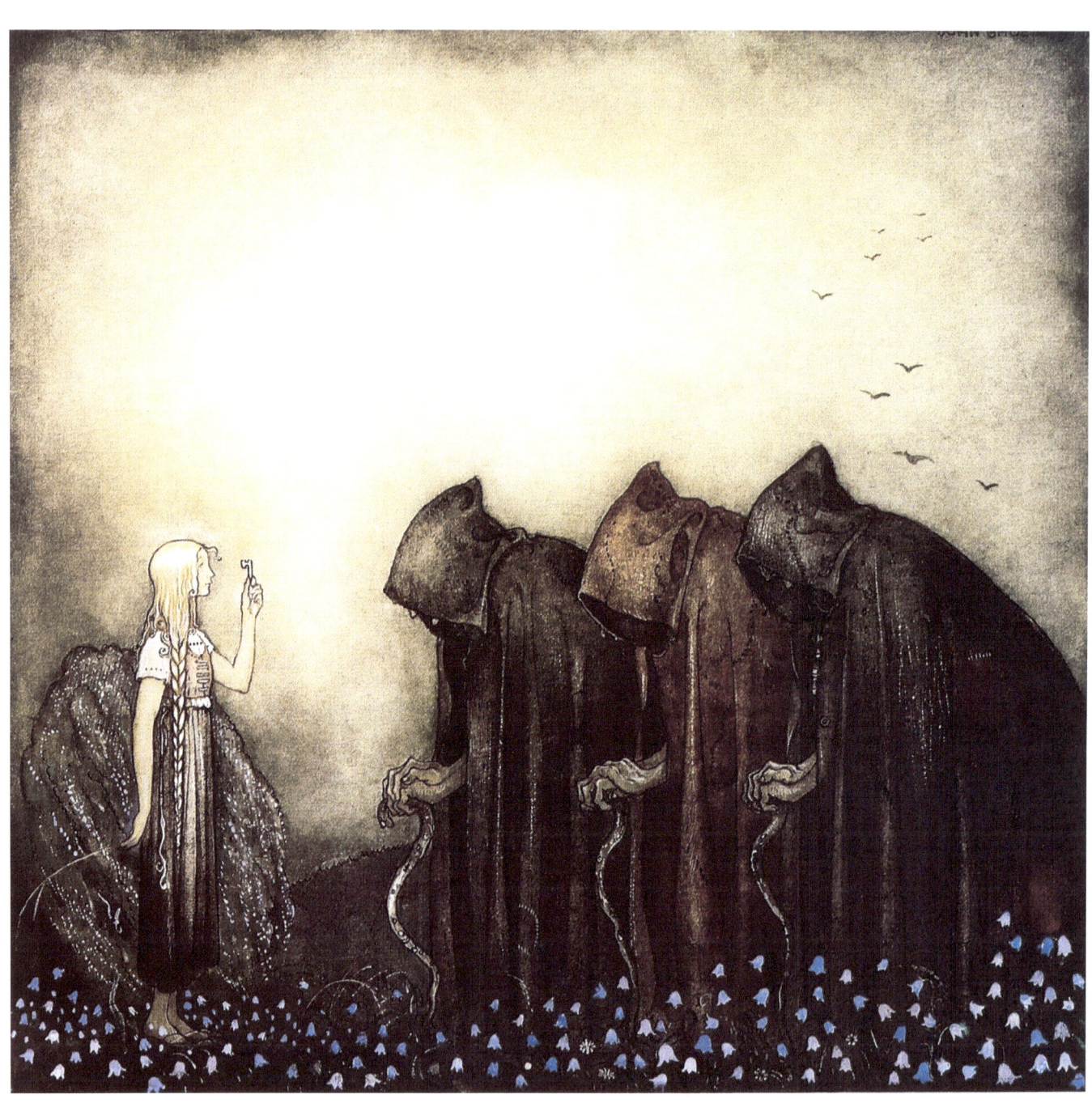

And she held up a key, a fine key made of pure gold.
From 'The Golden Key'

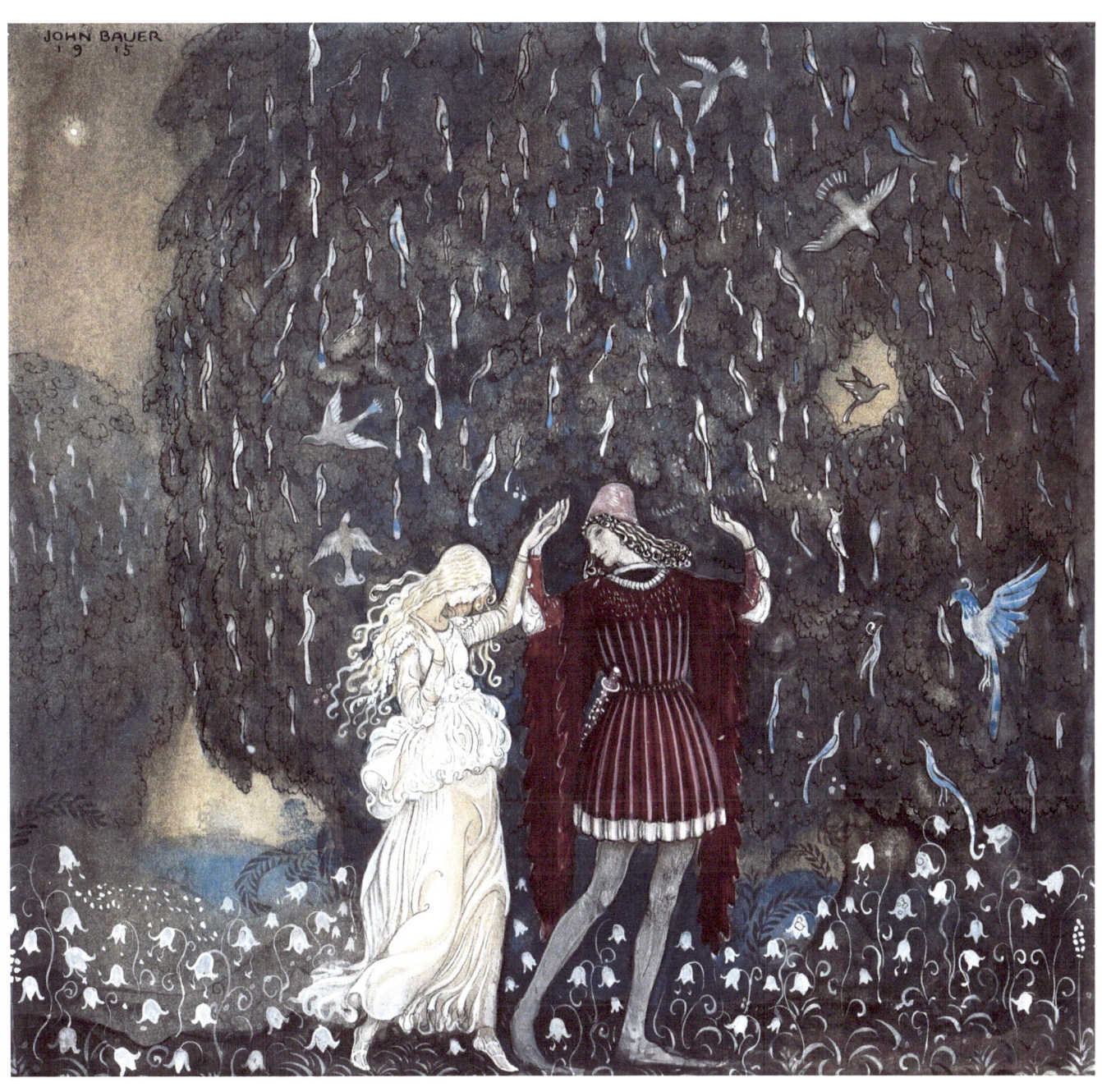

They danced on the meadow, and Lena sang, while she was dancing.
From 'The Golden Key'

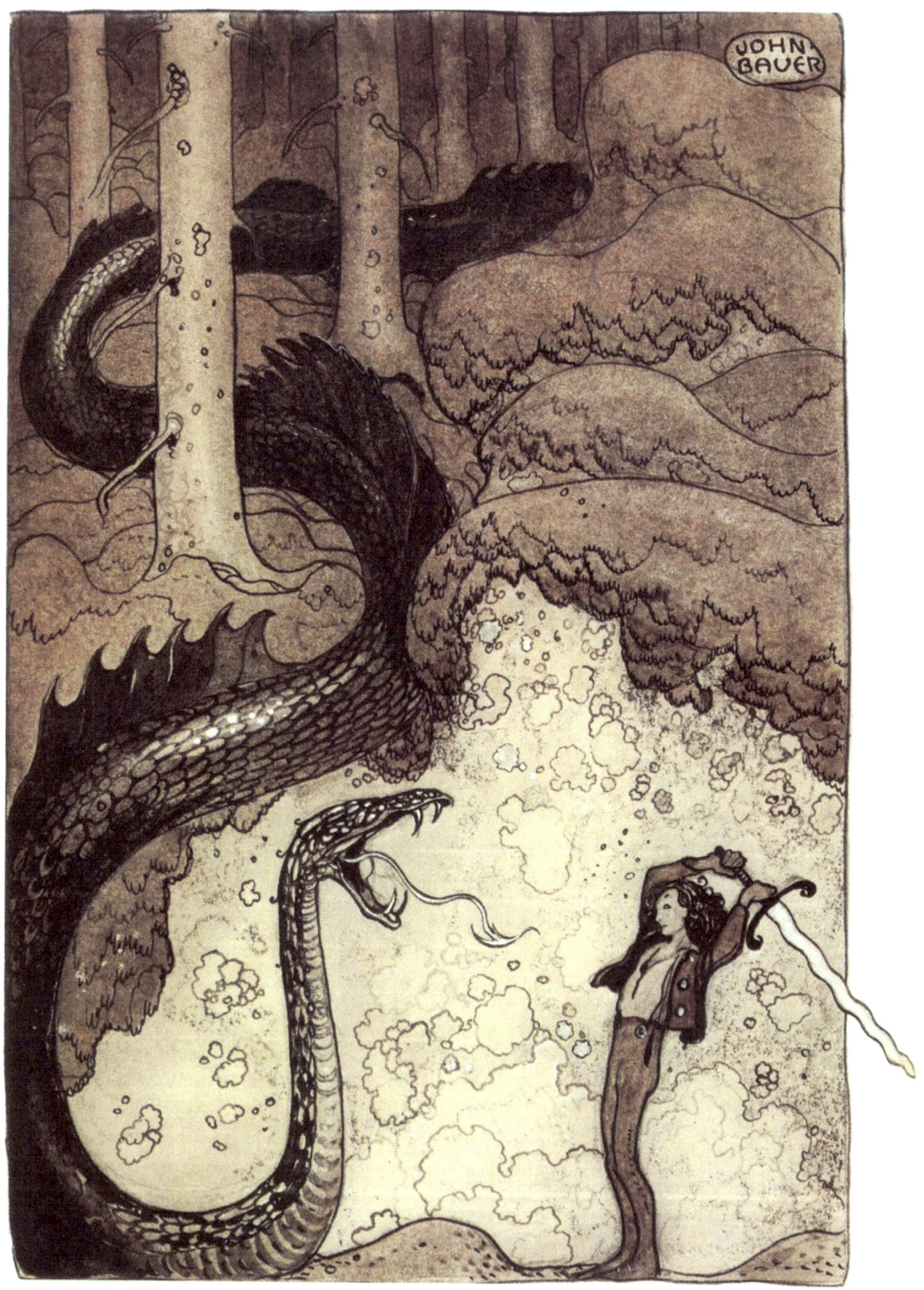

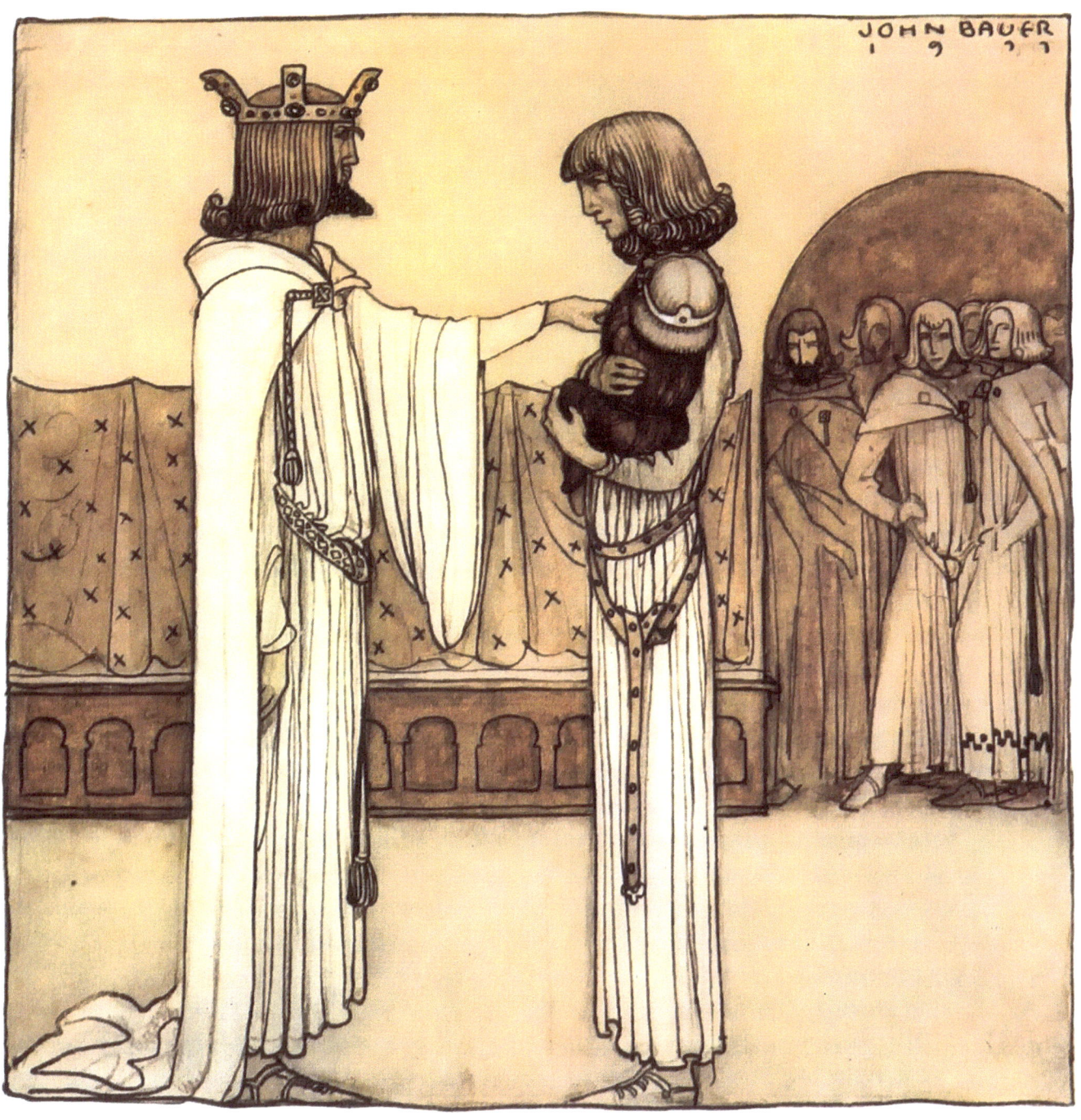

Above: The Kings Choice

Left: He gave the dragon a mighty blow.
From 'The Maiden in the Castle of Rosy Clouds'

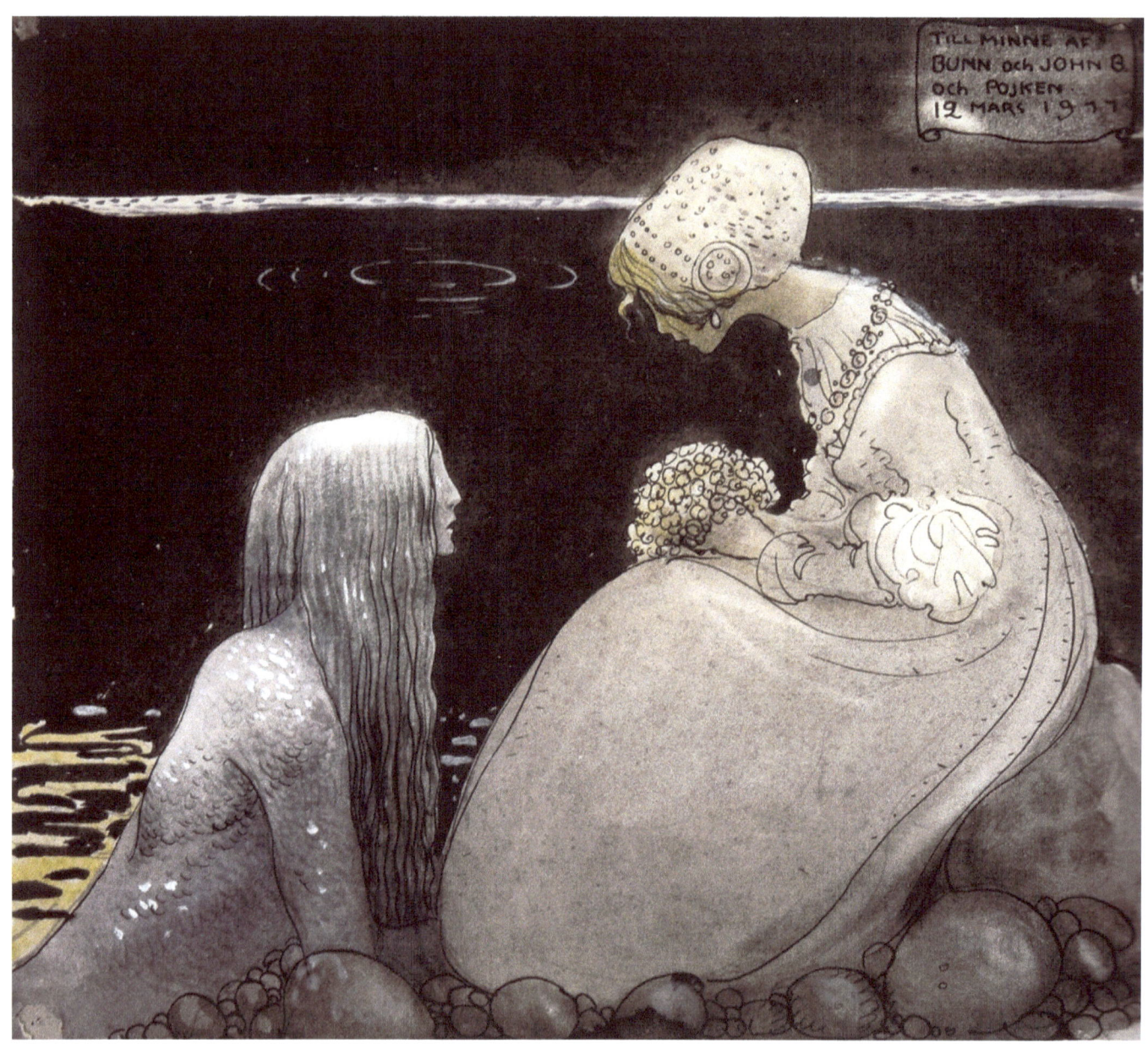

Above: From 'Agneta and The Sea King'

Right: From 'The Maiden in the Castle of Rosy Clouds'

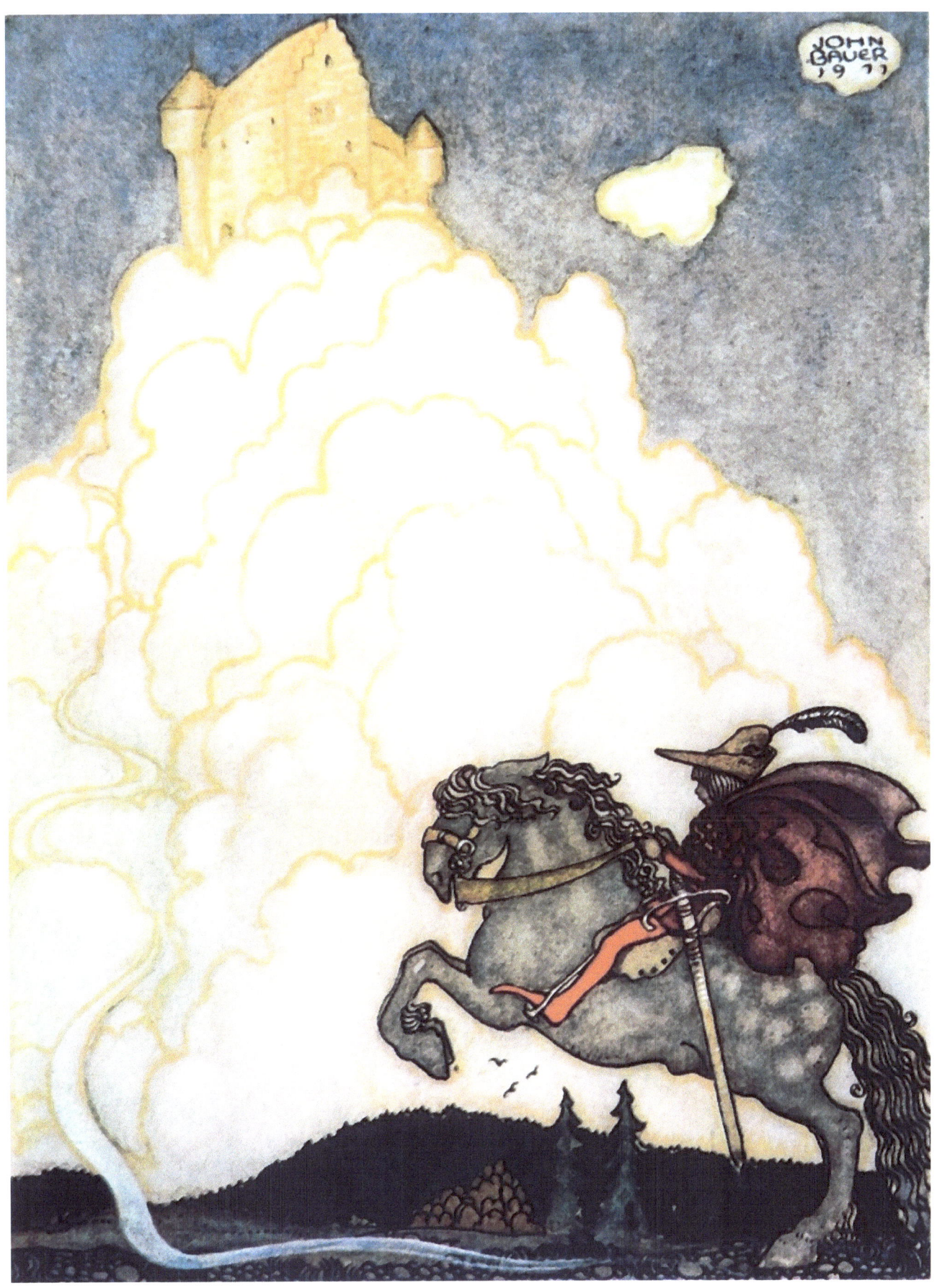

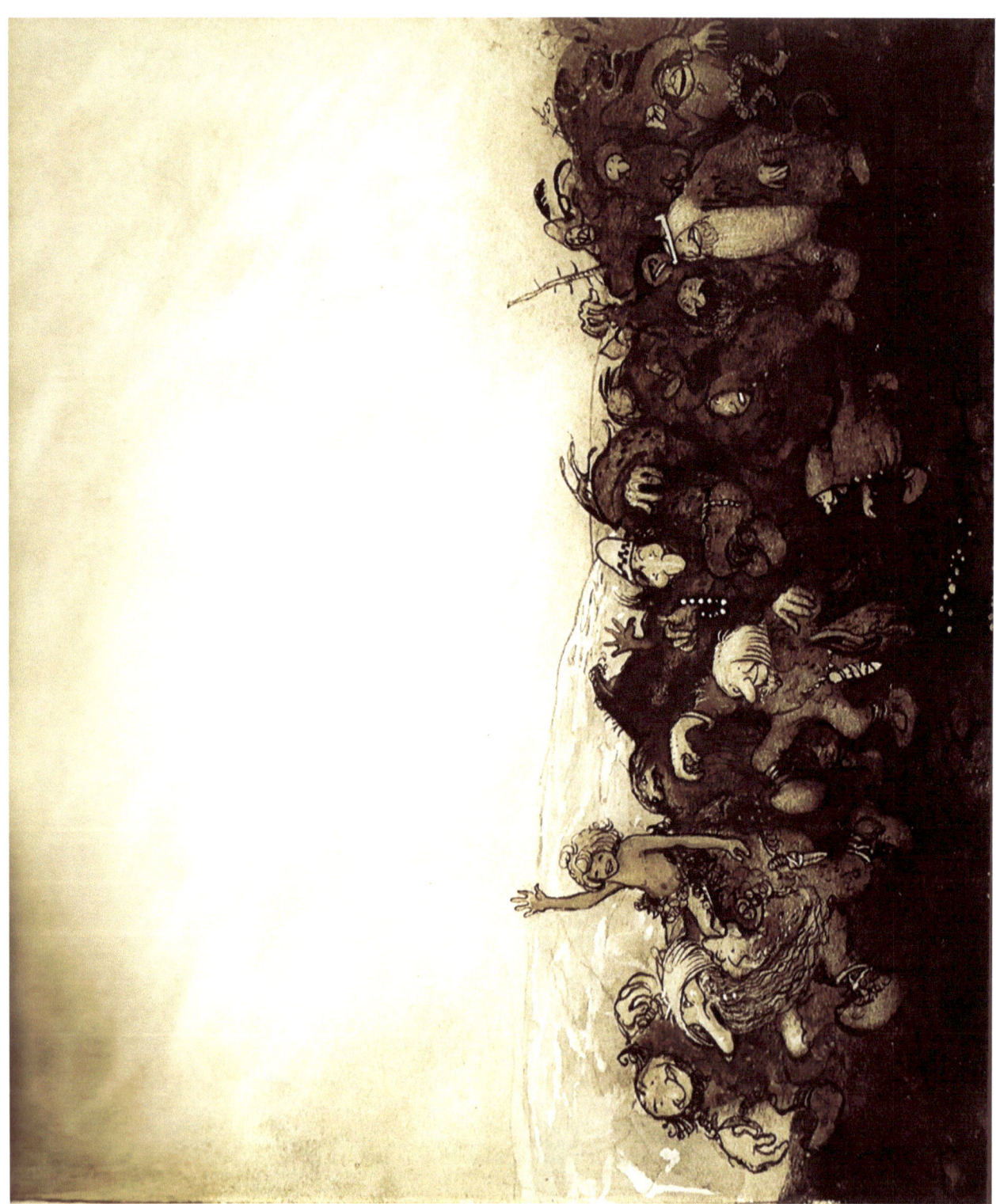

The Four Big Trolls and Little Peter Pastureman

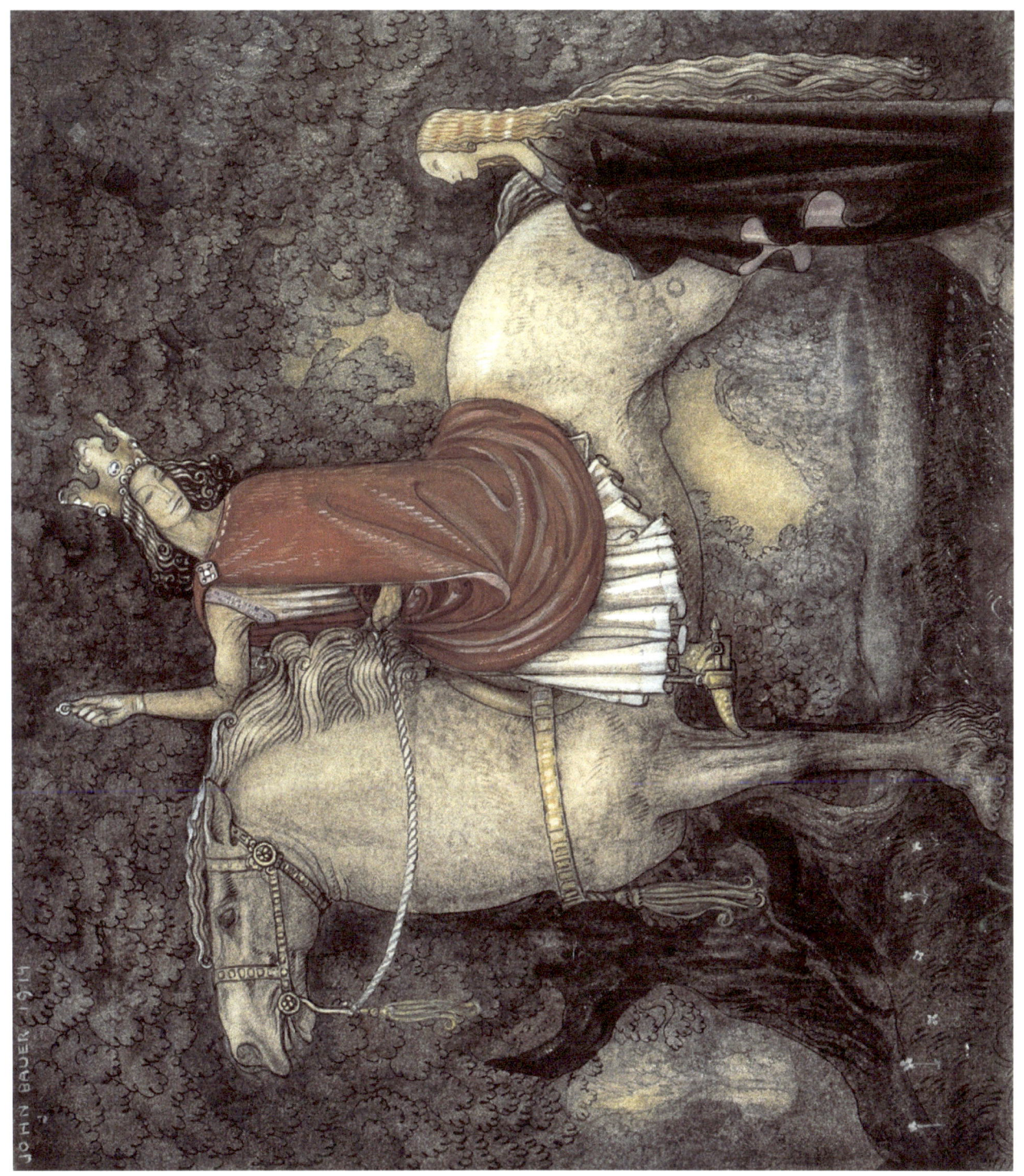

Once upon a time a young Prince went riding out in the moonlight. From 'The Ring'

When the Troll Mother took care of the King Storbyk

Riding out in the moonlight. From 'The Ring'

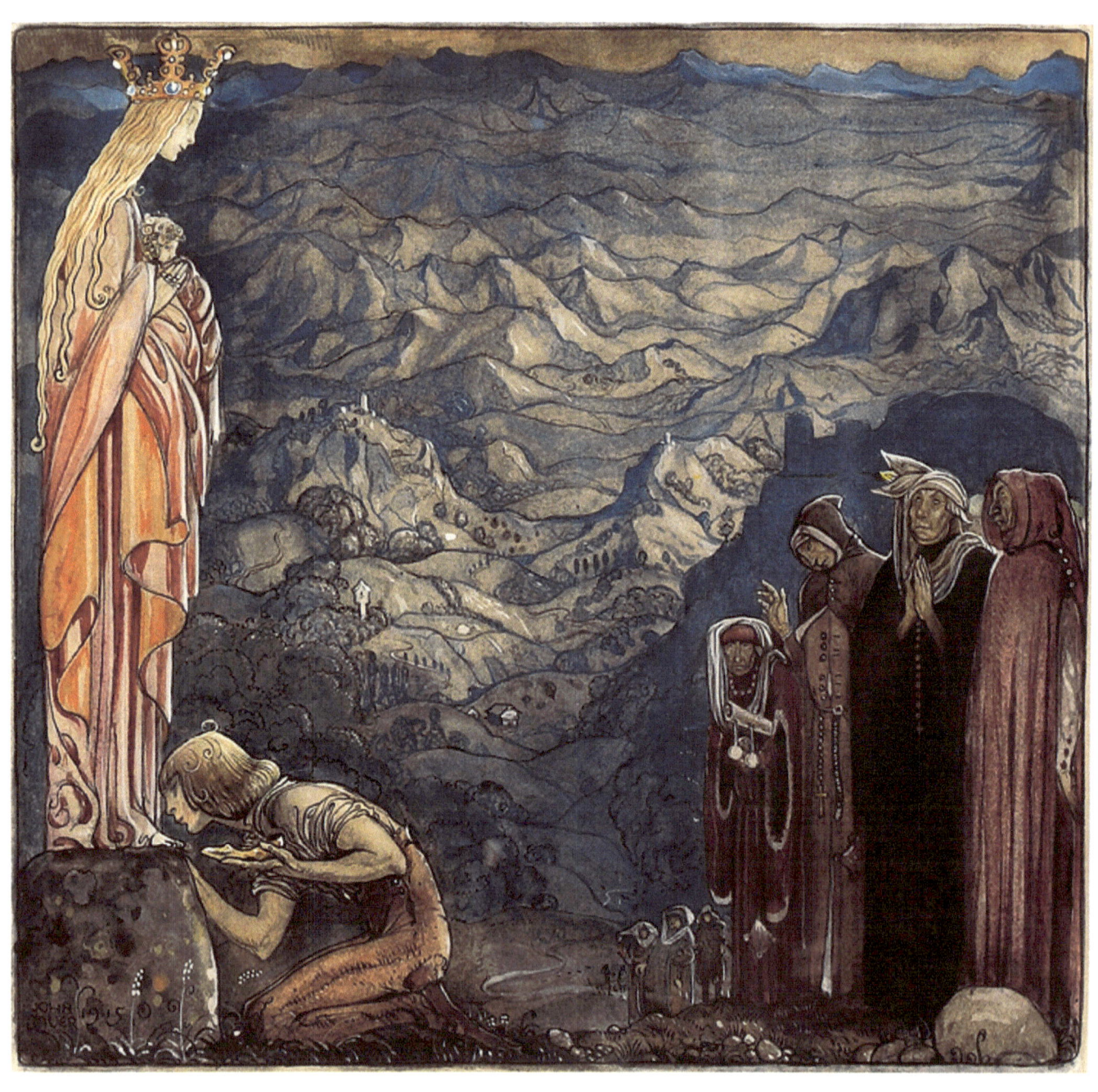

He stepped forward to the figure of Madonna and kissed her bare foot humbly.
From 'The Musician who got the Madonna's Gold Shoe'

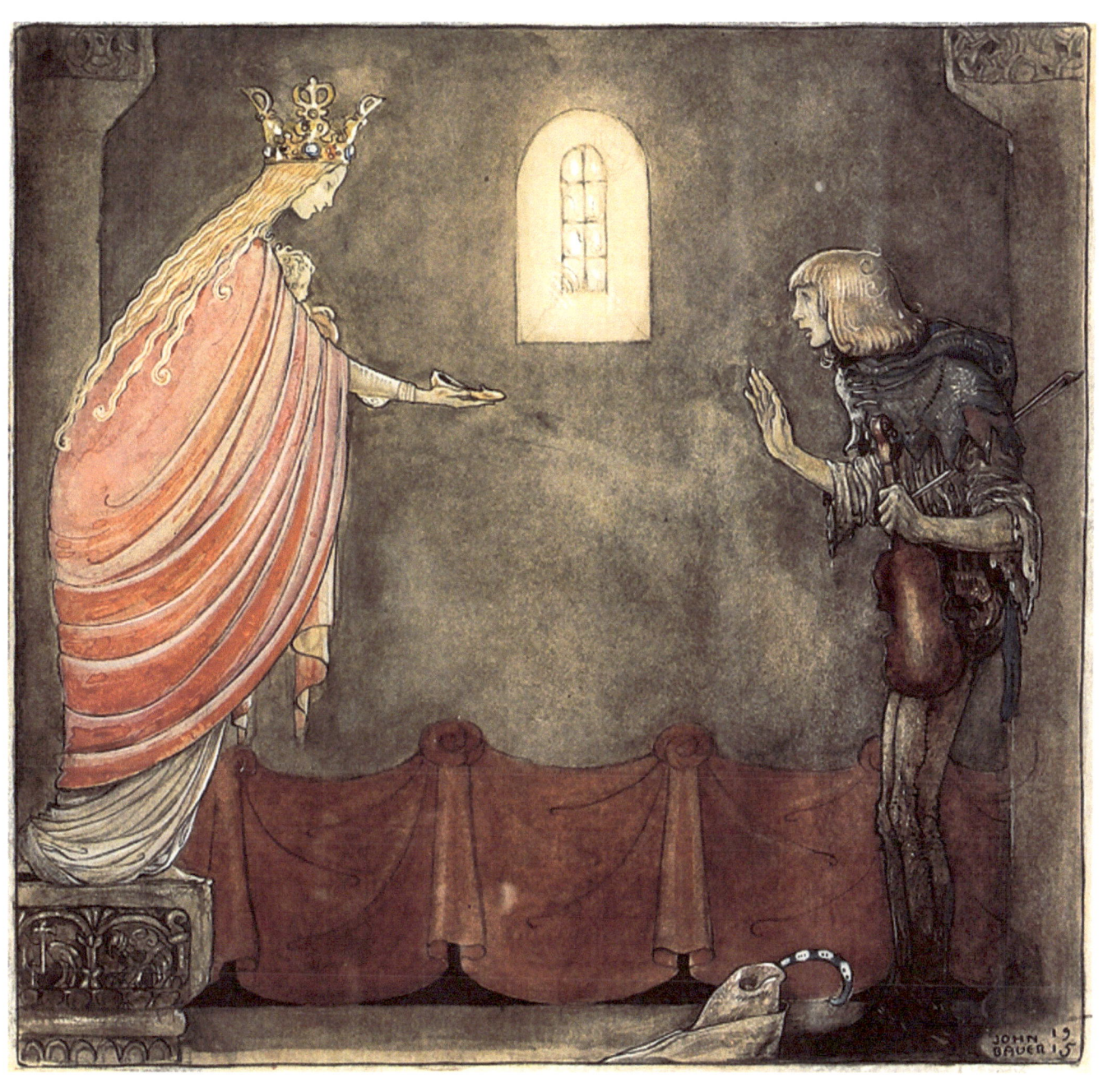

He saw the holy maiden bend down and take off one shoe and smiling handed it to him.
From 'The Musician who got the Madonna's Gold Shoe'

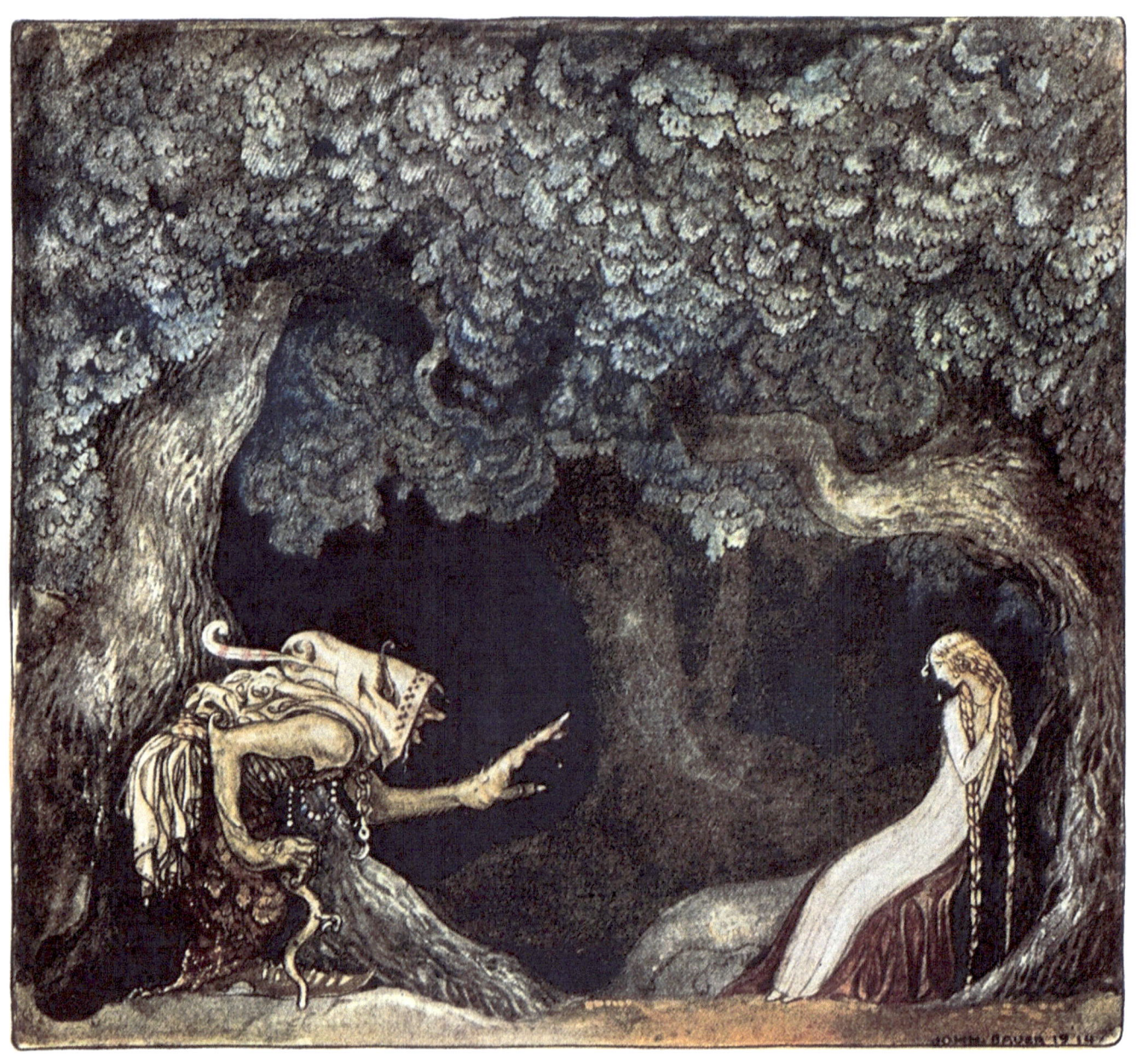

Above: The Queens Pearl Necklace.

Top right: Stalo and Kauras.

Center right: Sago.

Bottom right: The Trolls in Domberget await a Stranger.

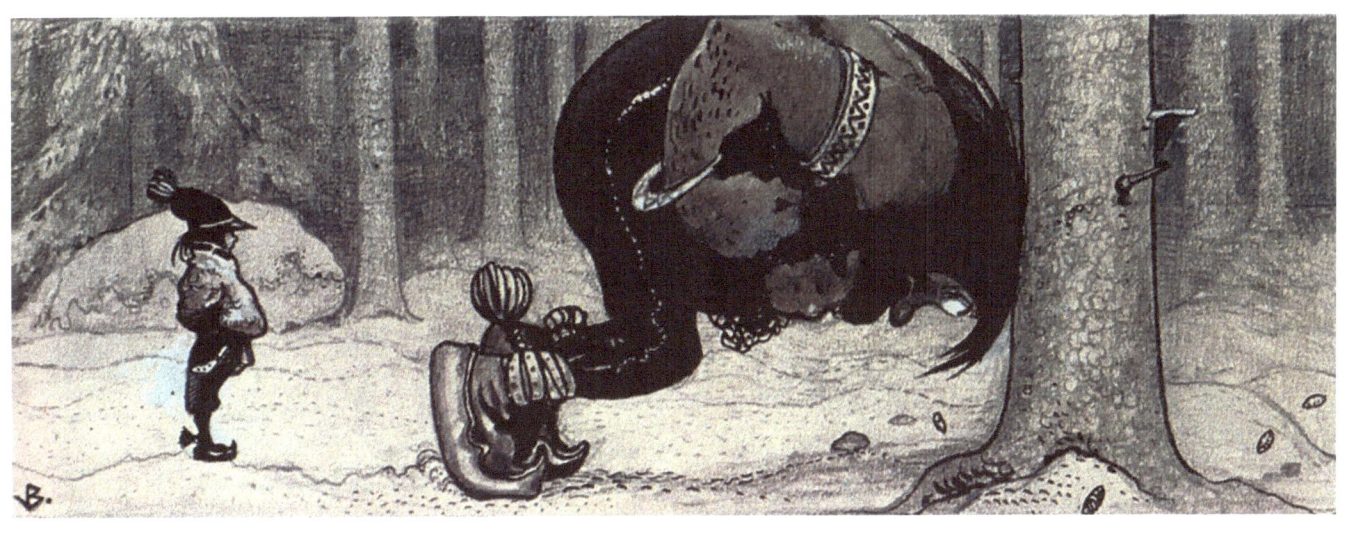
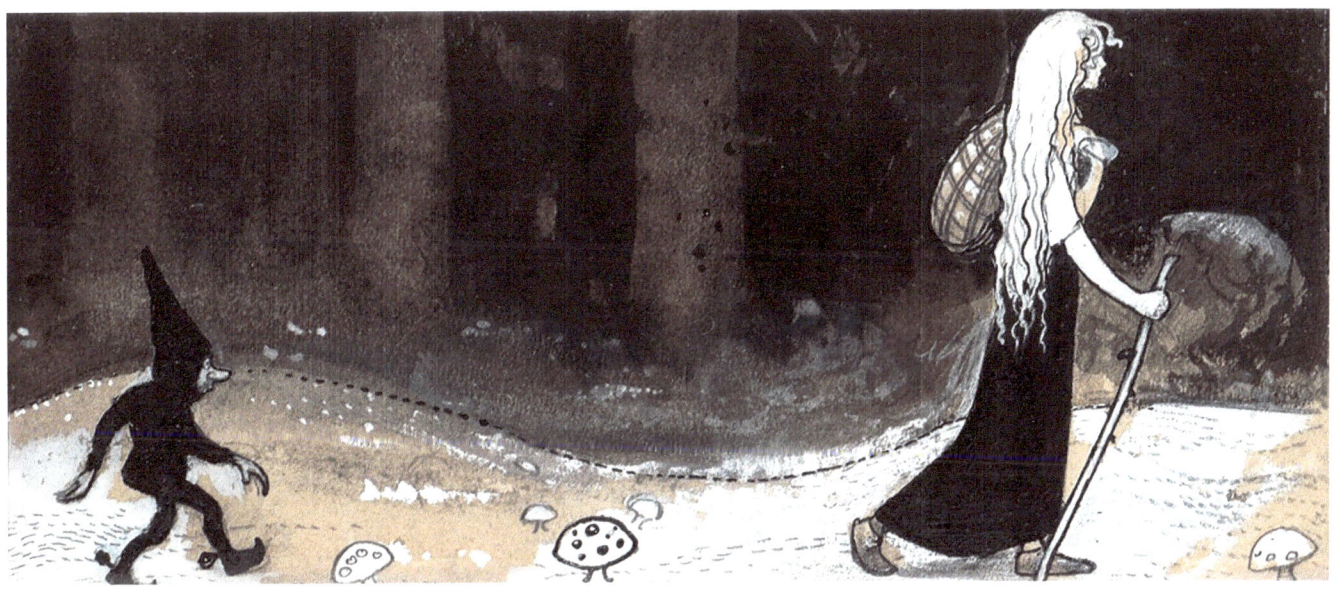
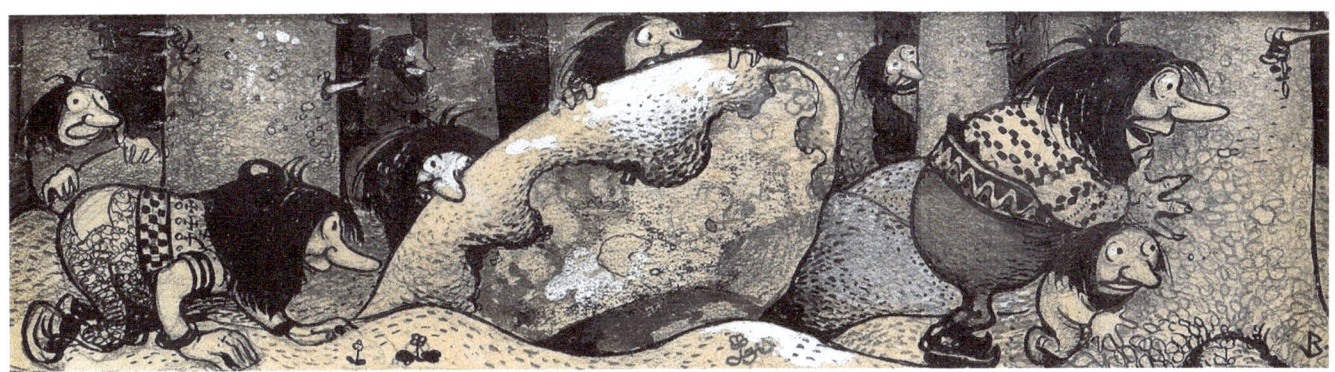

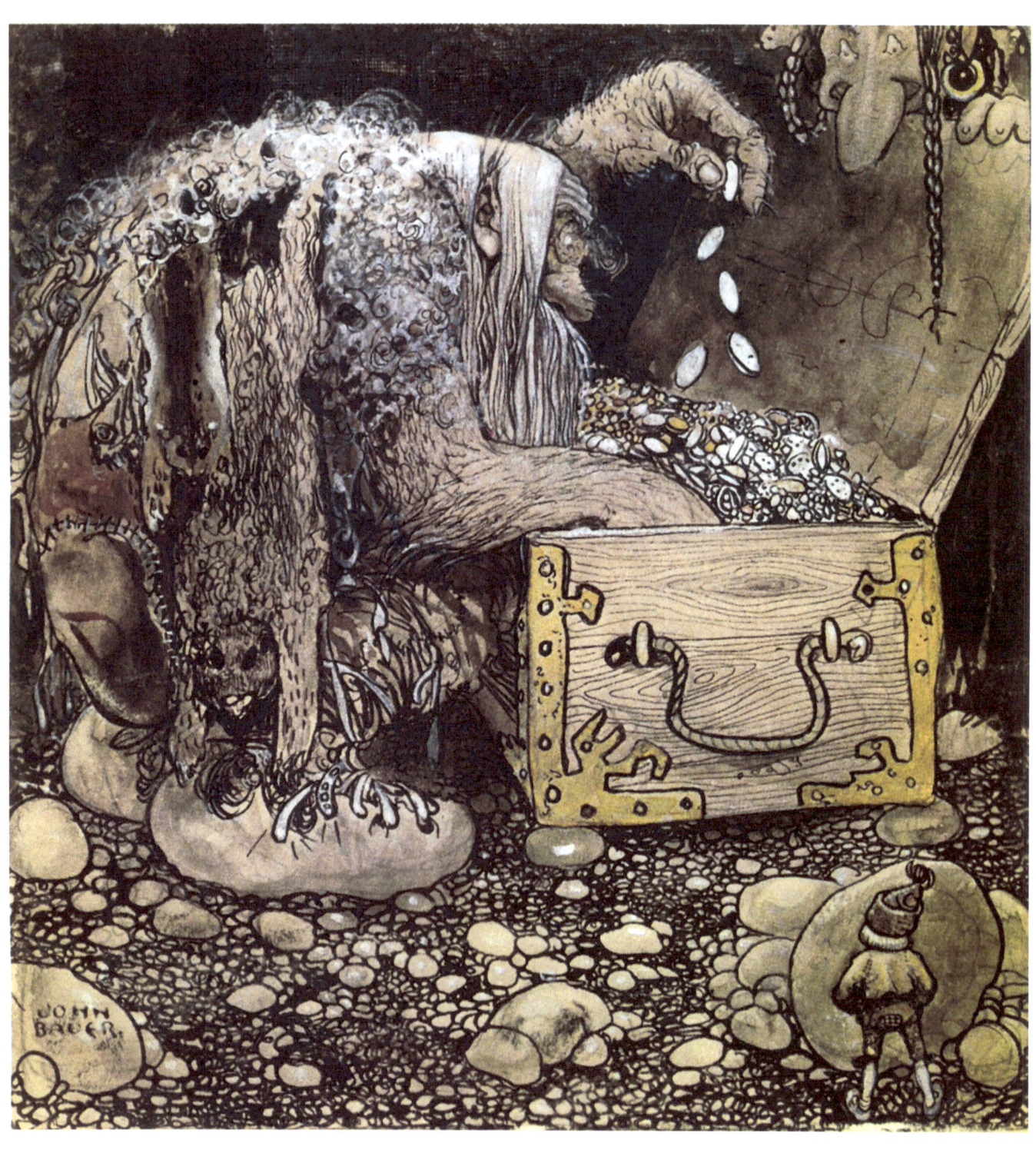

On the middle of the floor there was an open treasure chest and with two horrible trolls sitting.
From 'The Trolls and the Youngest Tomte'

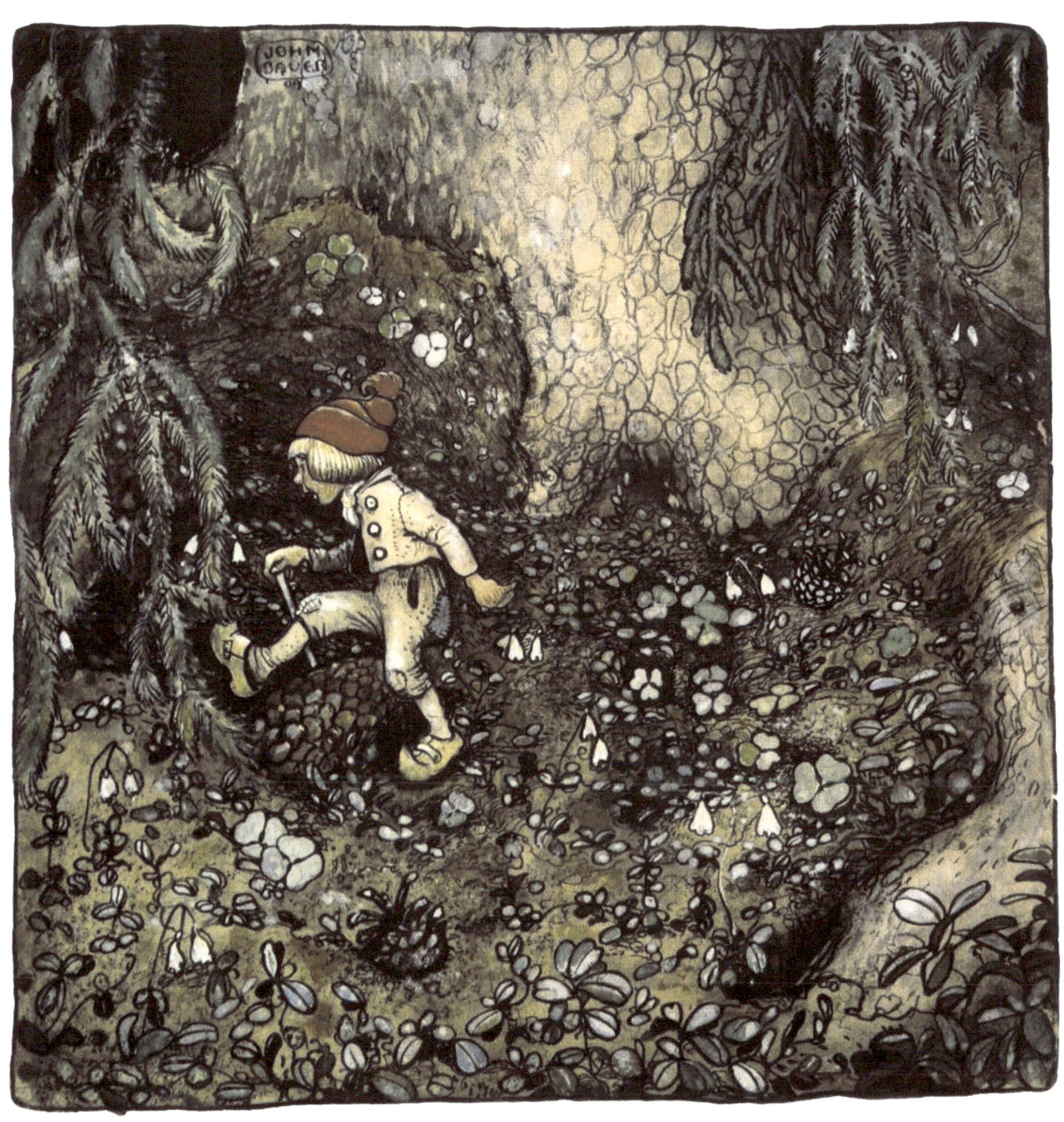

From 'The Trolls and the Youngest Tomte'

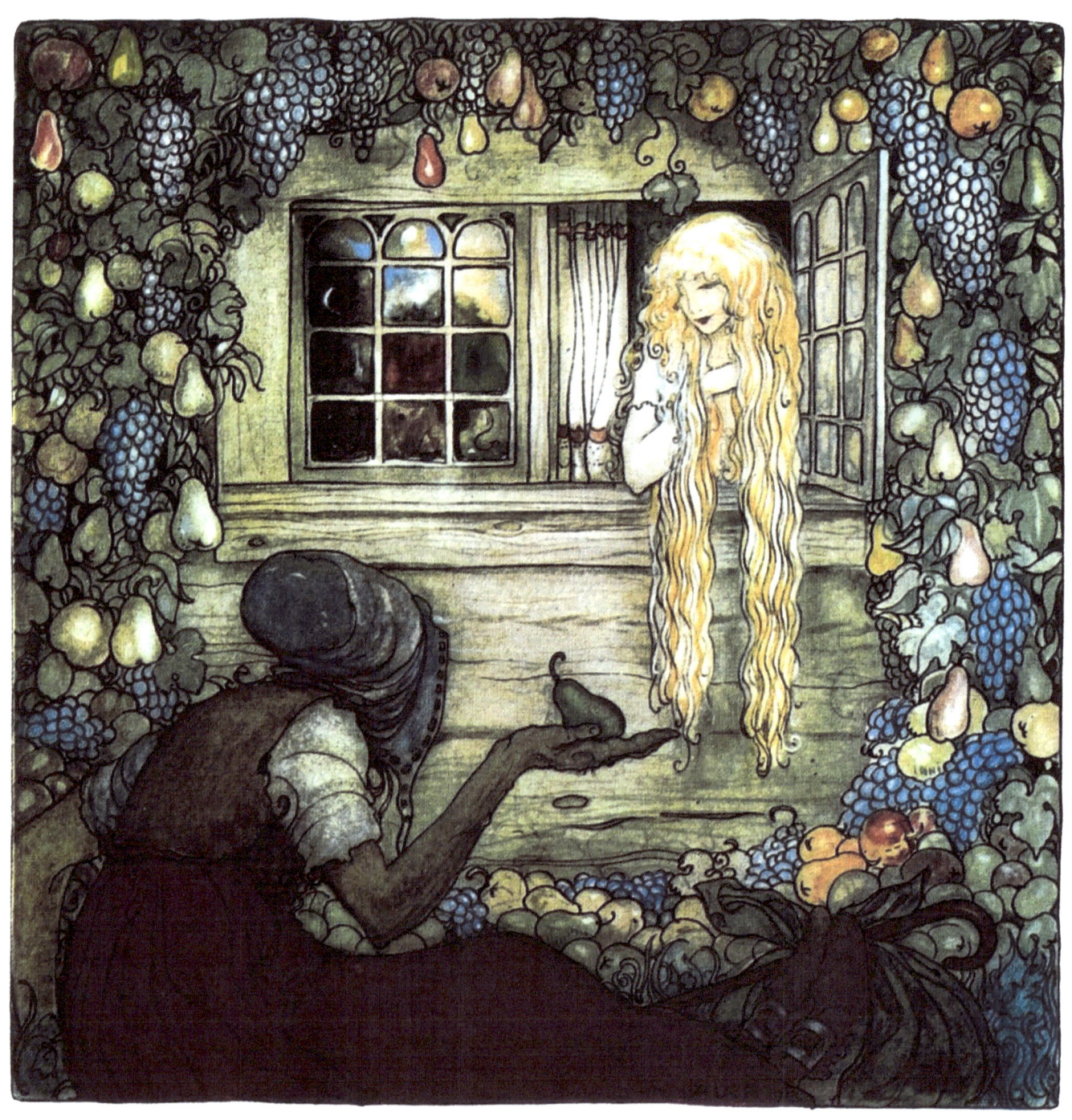

From 'The Wizard's Coat'

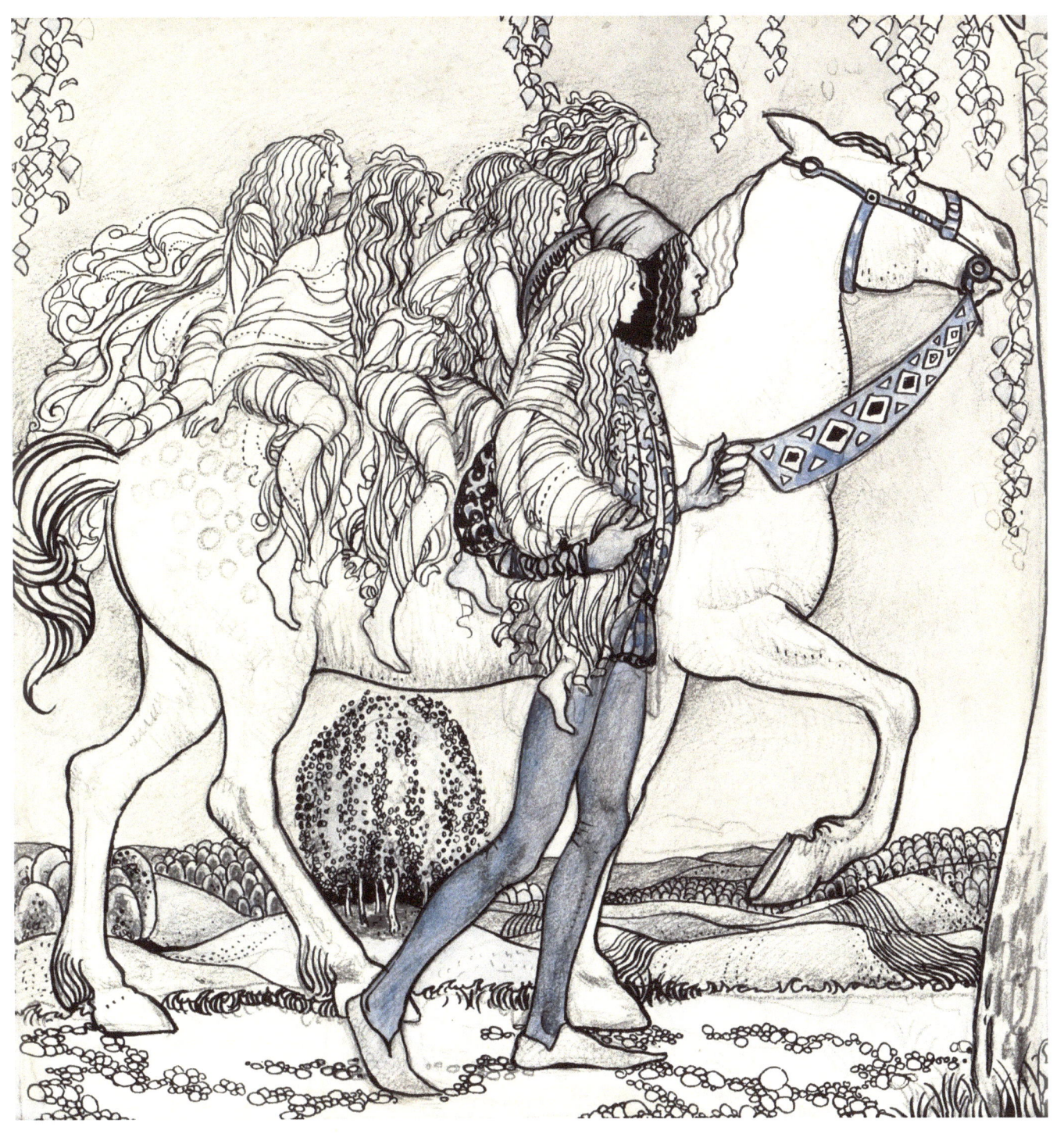

An unknown sketch

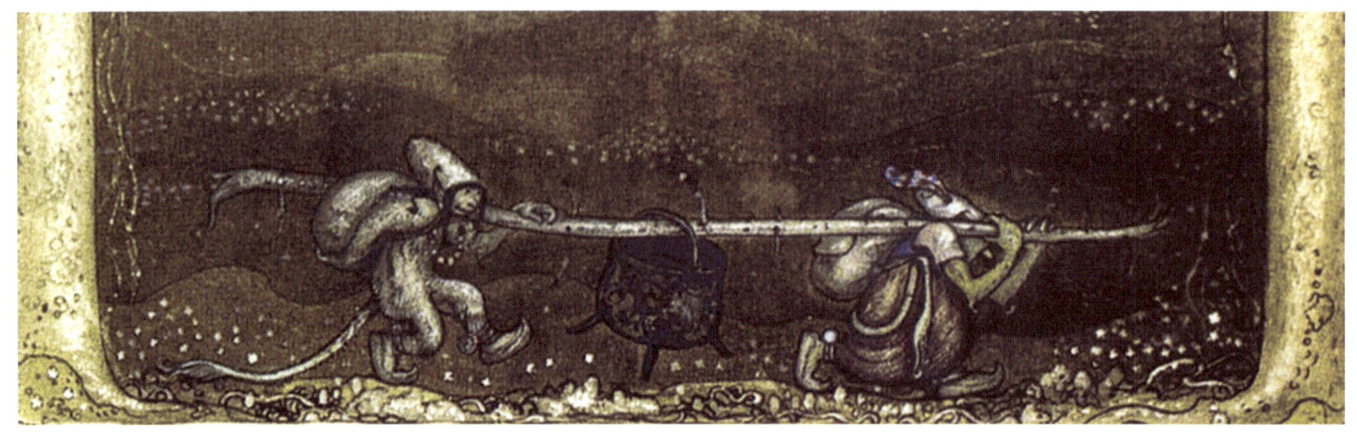

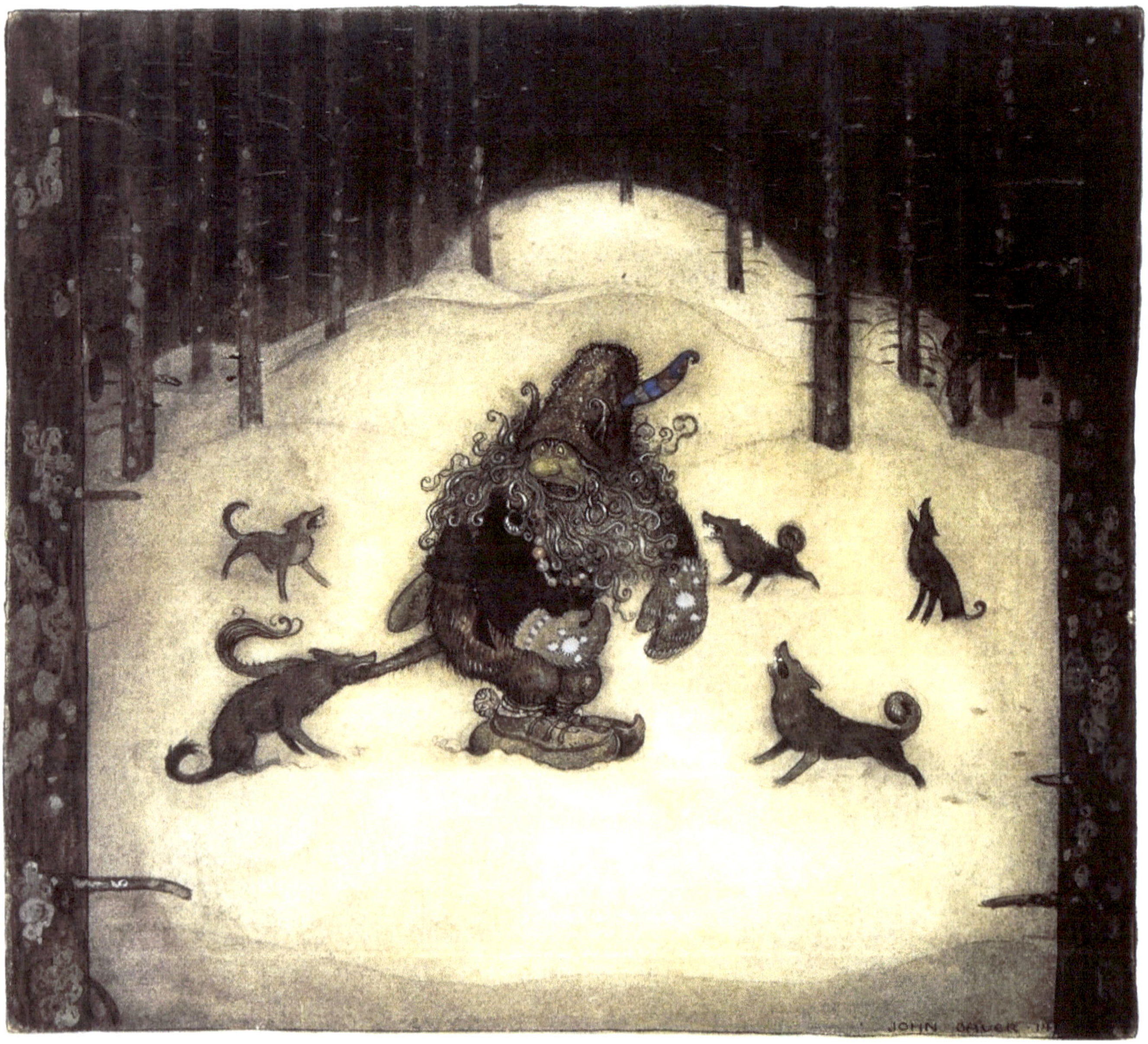

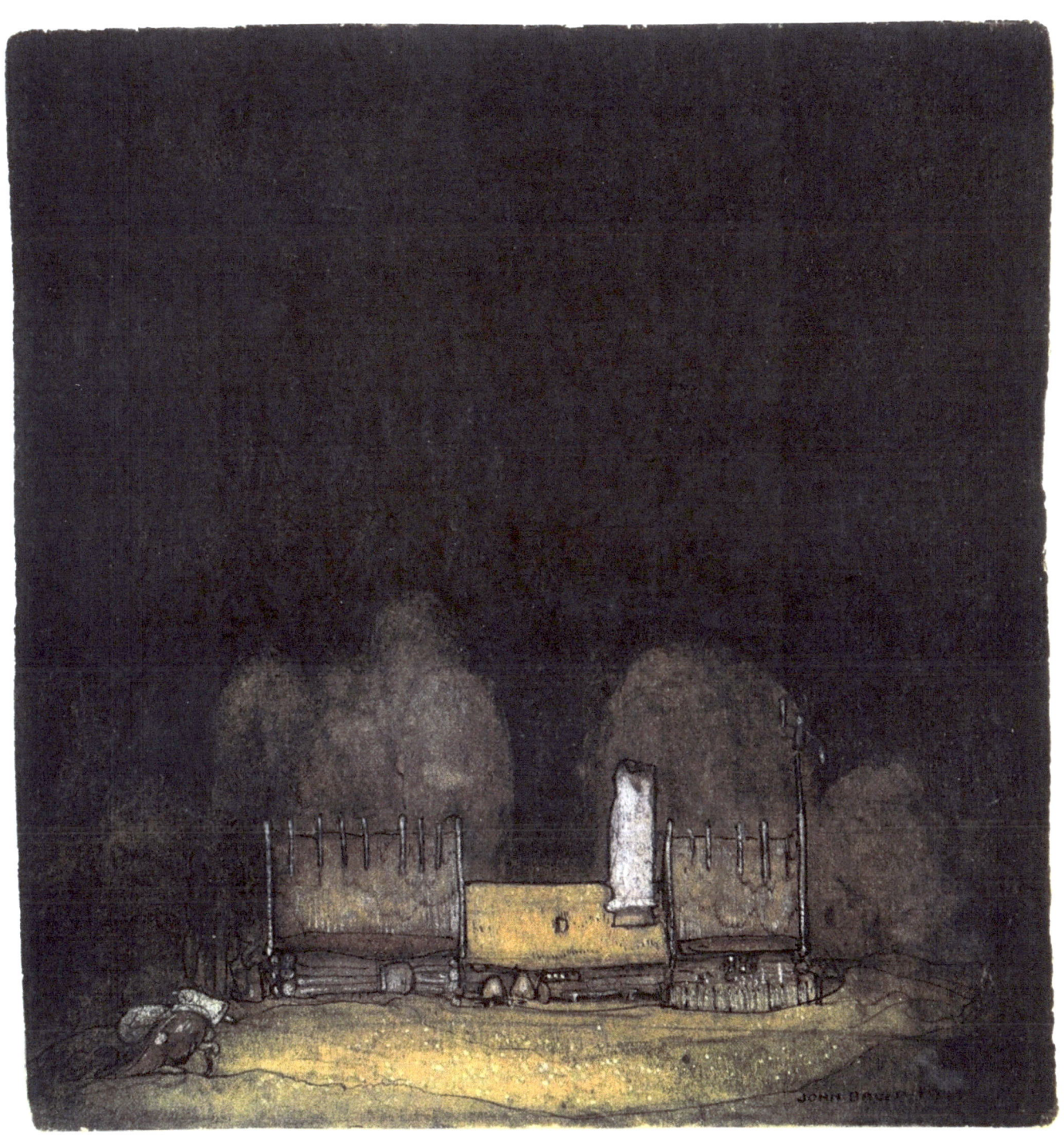

Above and bottom left: From 'When the Troll Mother took care of the King Storbyk'

Top left: When evening came, troll mother and the boy sneaked out of the mountain.

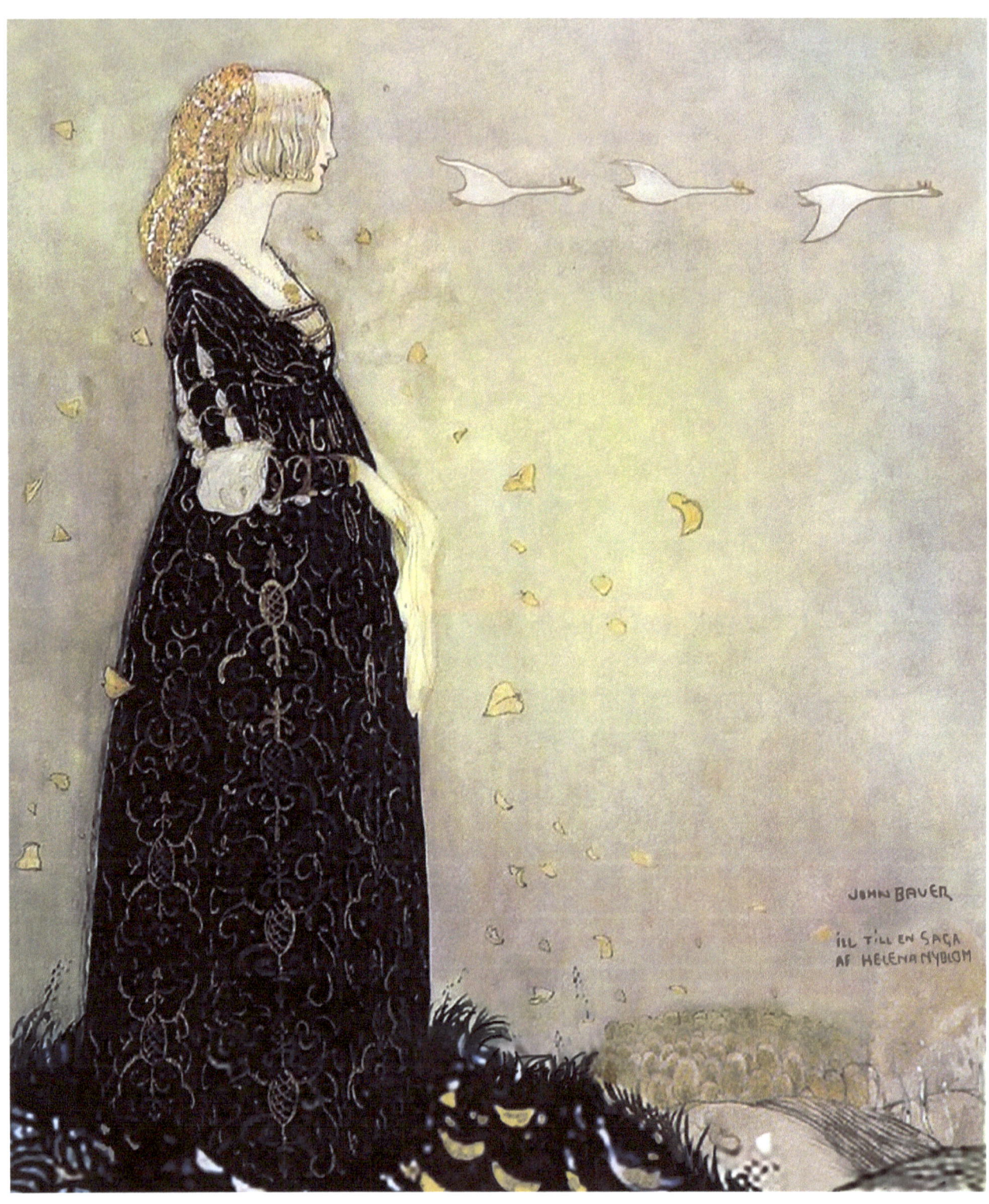

From 'The Swan Maiden'

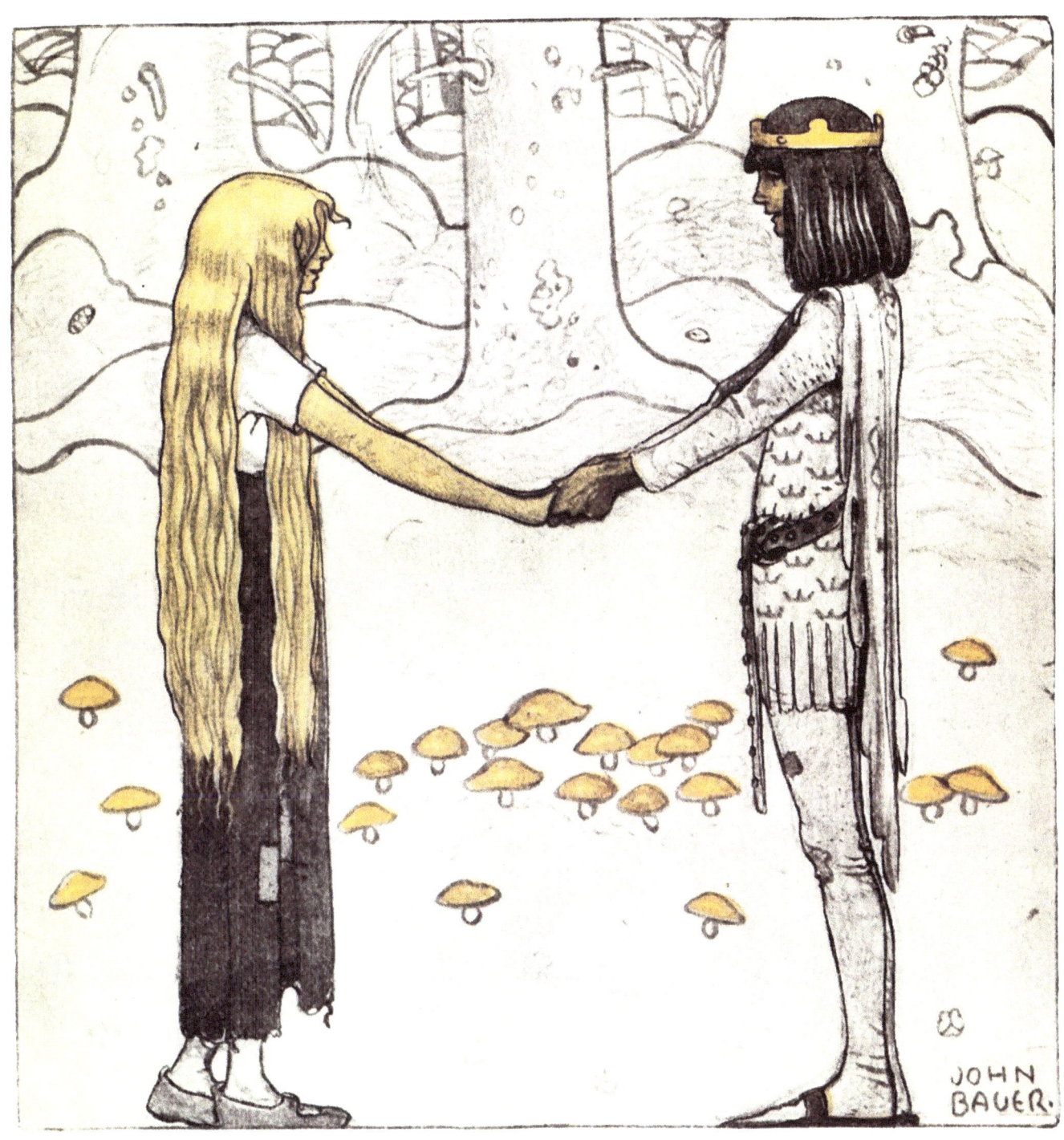

From 'The Shadowless Prince'

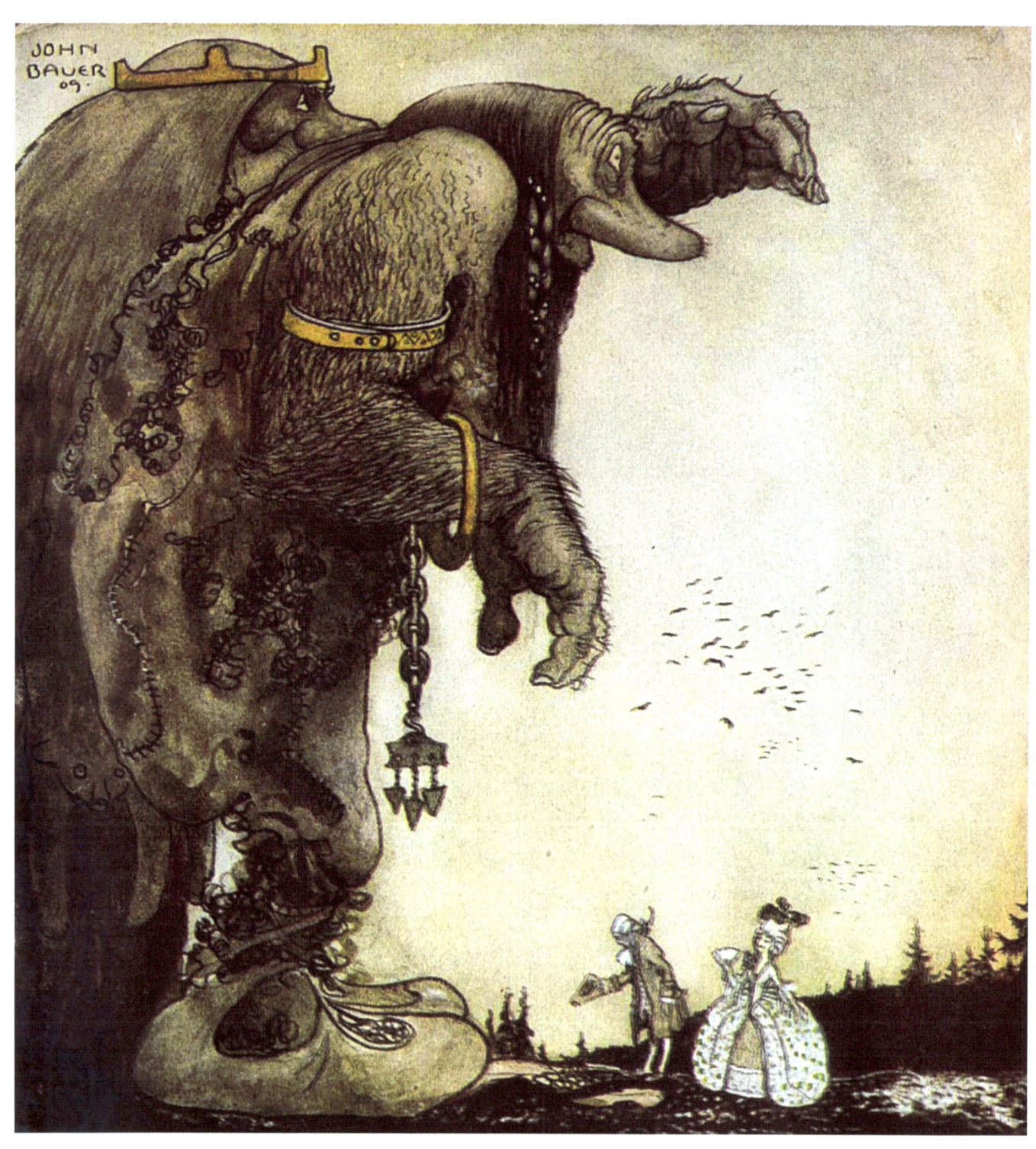

Two Giant Trolls

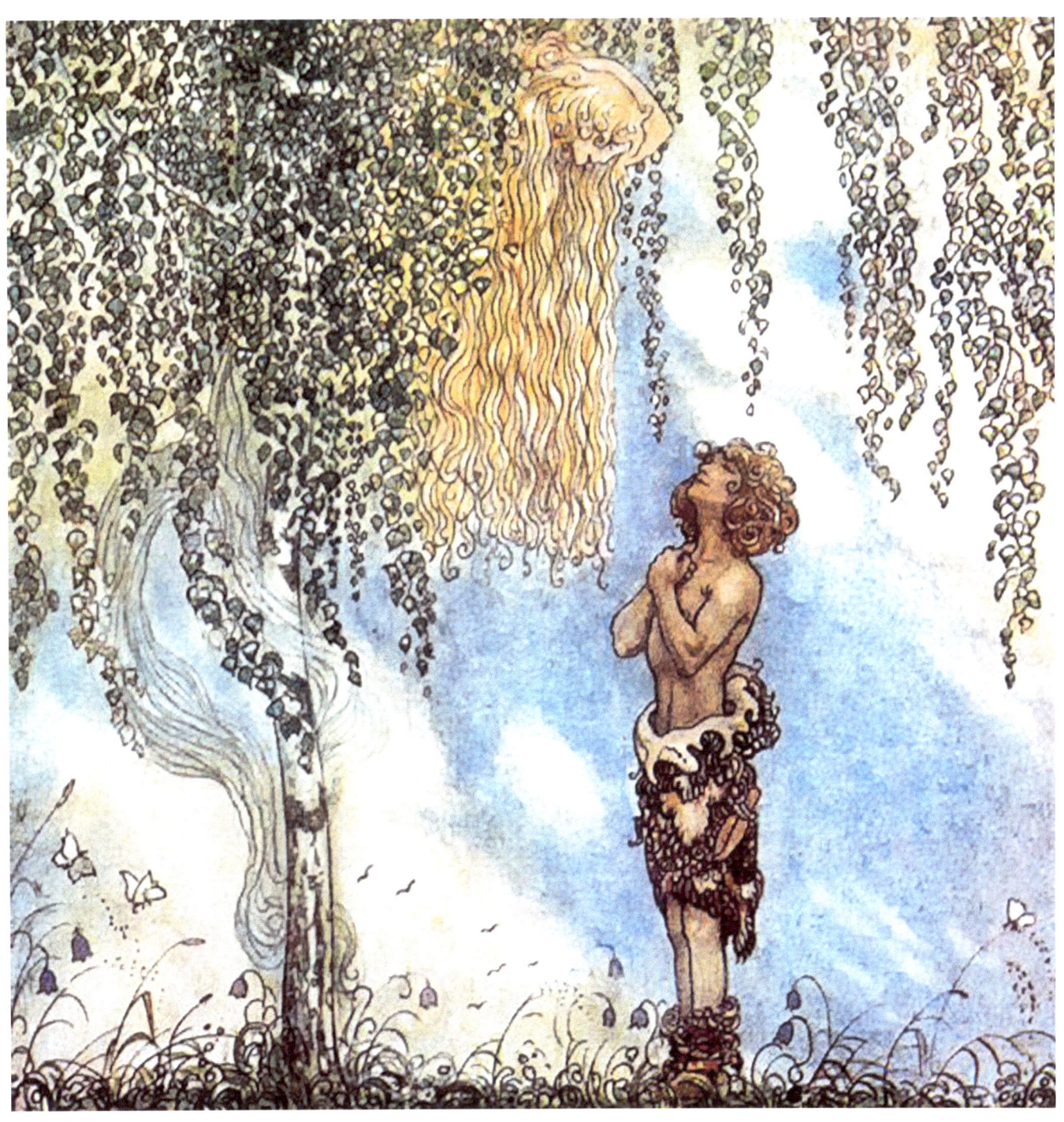

He saw her hiding in the tree.
From 'Humpe'

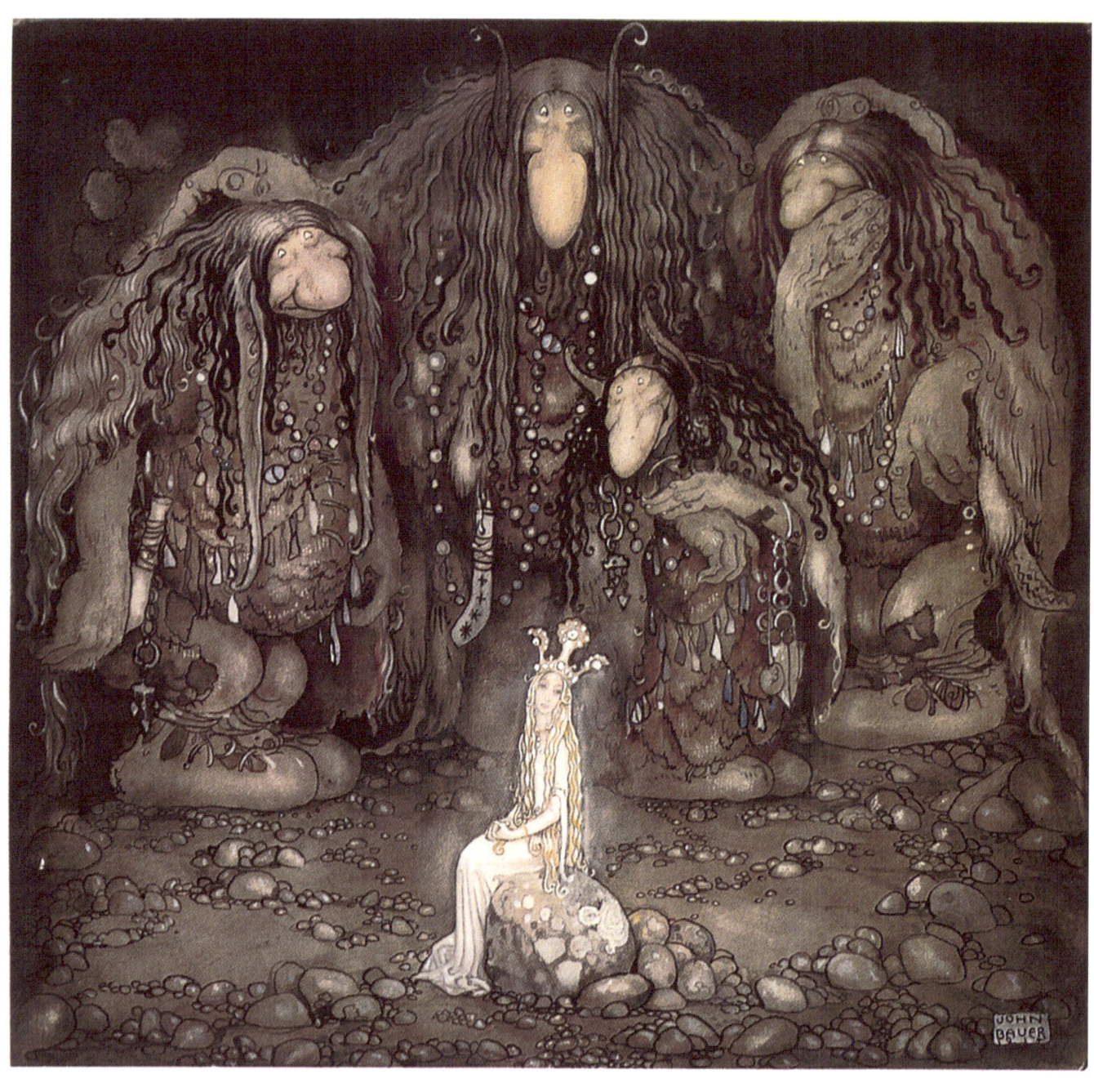

"Look at them," troll mother said. "Look at my sons! You won't find more beautiful trolls on this side of the moon."
From 'The Troll Mother Seeks a Wife'

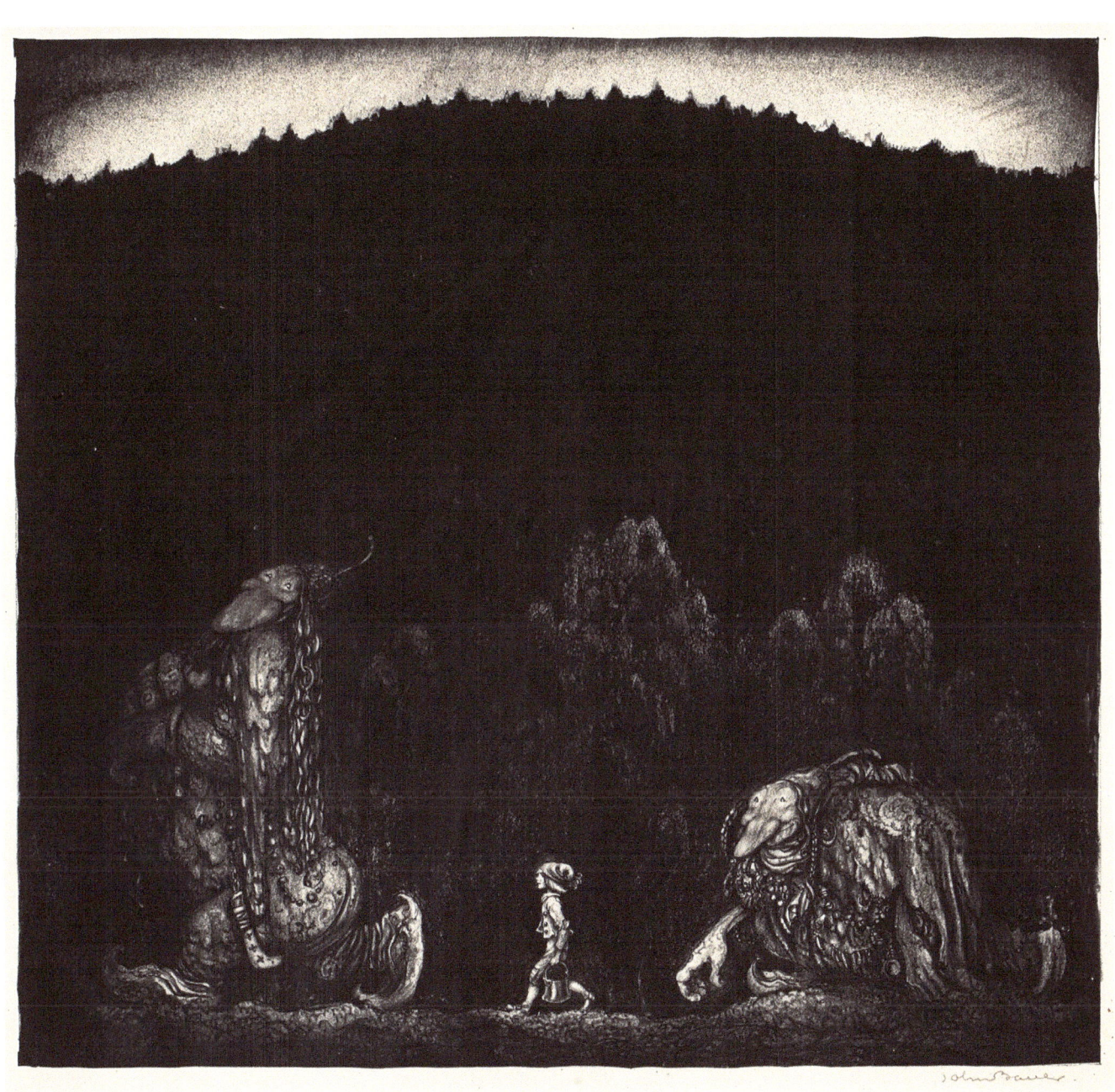

'Boy and Two Trolls' lithograph

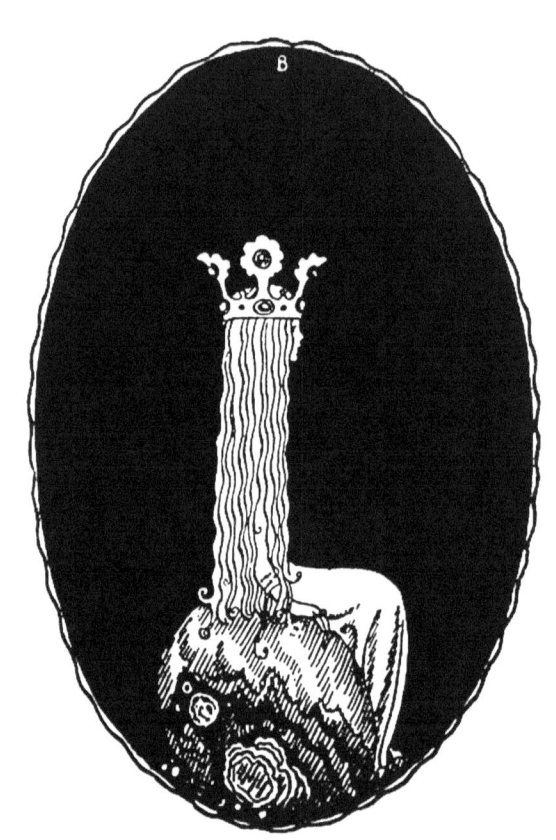

www.ingramcontent.com/pod-product-compliance
Lightning Source LLC
Chambersburg PA
CBHW051158220526
45473CB00003B/822